Hold Tight, Sweetheart

A Memoir of the Twenties and the Great Depression

U.T. Miller Summers

ভও ওও

For the two of them:
Mary Elliott Miller and John Brison Miller
and
for family, friends, and neighbors,
in and out of books,
who have walked with me
through a very long life.

Special thanks to William and Mary Anna Towler, publishers of CITY, Greater Rochester's Alternative Newsweekly, in which early versions of some chapters of this book were published. *Shenandoah* published an early version of "Bowling Green." The Rochester Institute of Technology publication, "Signatures," published an early version of "On Relief."

The cover and layout designer was Christina Hui. I am especially grateful to Mary Sullivan, RSM, who gave encouragement and advice.

With the exception of my two sisters, most of the people mentioned in the book are no longer living. A few fictitious names have been used.

Table of Contents

Chapter I

Hold Tight, Sweetheart

"No country, however rich, can afford the waste of its human resources. Demoralization caused by vast unemployment is our greatest extravagance. Morally it is the greatest menace to our social order." Franklin D. Roosevelt—Fireside Chat on Government and Modern Capitalism, September 30, 1934.

"Hold tight, Sweetheart. I'll make good yet." These words on a postal card addressed to my mother in late January 1936 were the last we ever heard from my father. The Great Depression claimed many victims and we believe he was one of them.

The postman delivered the card to Miss Gerta Young's house, which was around the corner from the Baptist Church in McKenzie, Tennessee. Mother, my two sisters and brother, and I had moved to three rooms on the second floor after the house on Spruce Street where we felt so at home had been sold. Before we moved, Daddy had already gone on the road in a new second-hand car.

The first time the door bell rang that morning the older woman who lived in the first-floor apartment answered the bell before any of us could get downstairs. At the top of the stairs Mother recognized the heavyset man in overalls on the porch as the garage owner from whom she and Daddy had bought the car. She called to him to come on up. By the time he made it to the second floor, the four of us were all gathered around her.

I would be sixteen on the last day of the month. Mary Elizabeth, the only dark-haired one among the blond-to-sandy-haired rest of us, was already fourteen. Caroline would soon be twelve and John B. was ten. Because it was too cold to hang around in the cotton flannel night clothes that Mother made sure we wore in winter we were all dressed and had eaten our breakfast of biscuits, gravy and canned peaches.

The garage man's face was kind under the cap he was wearing, but he was dismayed at seeing the four of us.

9

He asked Mother to step out into the hall. She motioned to us to move back and closed the door to the back bedroom behind her.

We did not leave the room because we knew that however much the garage man disliked speaking in front of us, Mother believed in telling children "anything of importance to the family" and would inform us later. The conversation between them was brief. Mother soon returned and told us that the Memphis police had called early that morning to report a car found on a side street of downtown Memphis not far from the Mississippi River. The name of the garage from which the car was bought was on the rear bumper and the garage owner recognized the four-door sedan as the car that he had sold to Daddy. The down payment with a $5 mail order sent his first week away would pay the cost of bringing the car back to McKenzie. Mother would be welcome to come to Memphis to pick it up.

Mother said, "I thanked him and told him 'No,' but asked to see anything left in the car." Though she was near tears she did not cry. She told us not to be worried, that she was sure "Daddy John" (our affectionate name for him) was "all right." Before he started out on the next round of job-hunting some time in the fall, he had told her that "to pull himself together," he might have to leave and not come back for a while.

For five Christmases since we moved to McKenzie in 1931, Daddy had come home with little or no money from trying to sell various items door to door or town to town. His down-heartedness was worse than his not making money. The worst was the Christmas just past. His previous wreck of a car broke down on the edge of town and the garage man said that it couldn't be fixed. That was why he needed the new second-hand car in which he had driven away.

When she heard that the car was being repossessed, Mary Elizabeth burst into tears, "I shouldn't have given that old garage man my chicken money. Now I will never get my bicycle." For part of the down payment Mother and Daddy had persuaded her to take out of the bank the money she had made raising chickens at our grandparents' farm.

"Yes," Mother said in a low serious voice, "You should have." The door bell rang a second time about fifteen minutes later. Typically Mary Elizabeth or John B. would have run downstairs before the woman on the first floor could get to the outside door, but they were both too troubled by the news to notice the ring. My memory is that it was I who hurried to the porch where the postman placed a single penny postcard in my hand. I climbed the stairs two at a time to hand it to Mother. She moved toward the light of the bedroom window to glance at it and then read it aloud. It was postmarked "Memphis" and dated the day before.

Daddy had been thinking of us as recently as yesterday.

"Do you still have that postal card?" Jackie Miller, the daughter of my brother John (he had dropped the "B" in his name as an adult), asked in a soft voice with a trace of a Spanish American accent. We were talking about Daddy at a family reunion a little more than sixty years after that earlier Saturday morning.

Except for a few family photographs and the two framed oil paintings from an art class at Teachers' College, most of our early possessions had been lost among the many moves Mother made after the children left home. For years she carried that postal card in one battered purse or another, but somewhere it was lost. The answer to Jackie's question was "No."

But even though the Chancery Court of Carroll County in Huntingdon, Tennessee, on October 4, 1957, declared John Brison Miller officially dead, more than twenty years after his disappearance, none of us entirely quit expecting that he might appear some time, just around the corner in one of the strange cities to which we traveled or among the faces in a restaurant, airport or bus station. Or walking at evening into one of the many places we have lived during the passing years—smiling, aiming to surprise us and looking just the way he did when he left at the age of thirty-nine—big nose, big Adam's apple, the same laugh wrinkles around his eyes, not a sign of balding or graying and even in those hard days, neat and well-dressed like a city man.

So now I intend to go back and tell the stories of my parents. Like so many other ambitious parents they left their family farms around the time of World War I with high hopes of making good in the outside world, she as one of the first woman ministers of her time, my father a little vaguer, but still determined to become the success that his family and neighbors expected. Having attained their college degrees after the birth of four children, they ran head on into the Great Depression.

In the hearts and minds of the children, the Depression was not so much deprivation as it was our parents' deep sense of failure. In their era of bad times, intelligence and hard work were not enough. We also discovered that good times were almost as unpredictable as bad. What seemed like miracles could happen. We had no more intelligence than they and much less stress. But much of our good fortune in different times came our way because John Brison Miller and Mary Elliott Miller were who they were, both of them.

Be Somebody

Be like Other People. Like Grandmother and Granddad. Like somebody in a book. Like the girls at school. Like the other boys.

Be a nobody. Not like people. Like a sharecropper. Like somebody from the country. Like somebody raised in a barn. Like somebody who never had anything. Like somebody who never had any rearing.

Be a success. Make a success. Amount to something. Make good. Get to the top. Make your mark in the world. Be an artist, minister, writer, businessman, musician, scholar, the President of the United States, the president of Bethel College or Western Kentucky State Teachers' College or any president. A banker.

Almost from the time we were born, words like these clickety-clacked in our ears like the wheels of a train turning over or the crack-crack sound of the cradle rockers. The admonitions and warnings expressed our parents' ambitions and fears for us, even though three of the four were girls. They also expressed their hopes and terrors for themselves; they weren't too old to dream.

Both my mother and father had been valedictorians of their classes in high school. Maybe that is what brought them together. It was the first time either had met anyone with similar background who had their brains and ambition. But the early victories were huge loads to carry. They didn't want to disappoint the people who had had faith in them. Mother thought of Grandmother who had plucked the feathers of her thirty-seven geese three times and carried them on old Moll, the mule she rode, to sell in Enola and buy clothes for mother's first year at high school. Daddy remembered the man to whose house he rode twenty miles on horseback so that he could borrow his encyclopedia, volume by volume. He borrowed a volume a week, read it from the first page to the last and rode back to return it. The old man had had to fight his wife to make her let him bring that set of books across Texas in the covered wagon, and Daddy's reading it proved he was right.

None of us would have wanted applied to us Mother's phrases indicating the undesirability of conformity: "run with the crowd," "just like everybody else," "no individuality," "fear of being yourself." But we did want to have certain things that certain other people had and to do things they did.

Among the six of us, grown and growing, we varied in how much comfort and convenience mattered, and we all talked down "material-mindedness" and "selfishness" from the time we knew the words. We also knew that possessions figured somewhere in the prestige, the meeting of expectations, the expression of love that we all longed for.

Two Valedictorians

Mother saw her childhood as one long struggle to get to high school. She was born August 8, 1892, the eldest daughter in the Elliott family of one boy and five girls.

As the family story came to her, her Grandfather Elliott had been well-off, owned horses and had slaves back before the Civil War in which he favored the Union side. He lost his wife with the birth of the next baby after Granddad, his debt-encumbered land and his slaves at the end of the Civil War, and his own life soon afterward. Poor little shirt-tail Charley didn't have a pair of britches to his name. He grew up to show his good blood and good sense by choosing for a wife my grandmother, Nancy Elizabeth Cummins, among the seven tall daughters of a neighboring farmer. The relatives who had never taught Charley much but work loaned him some of the money to buy a farm in the rough back country of western Kentucky and went on his note at the bank for the rest. They and the bank had to be paid back with money made from pigs, cows, and any crops except the big money crop, tobacco. Granddad decided early on not to spend his life raising tobacco—"something that was no good to anybody." The fact that he chewed it himself made him that much more determined.

There was a backbreaking amount of work to make the farm pay for itself: to keep wood and water in the house, the fires going, the meals coming to the table, the cows milked, and the family clothes washed and ironed. Mother was a worker. When she was four years old, Granddad put a wooden box up to the kitchen table so she could reach it to wash dishes. Soon she was frying meat and eggs and making bread. Then as Aunt Edna came along to help in the house she began working out in the fields with Granddad and her older brother, Henry.

Granddad always let them lay off the corn chopping to go down to the river and wave at the river packets which churned by two or three times a week. But Mother was fast and stayed at the chopping better than Uncle Henry. Granddad said years later he

15

didn't know whether he ever would have paid for the farm if she had gone to high school when she finished grade school instead of staying at home to help until she was eighteen.

Feeling his own education so neglected, he told Mother as they chopped corn side by side that if he had it to do over, he wouldn't have stopped this side of Harvard or Yale. He would have learned half a dozen languages and to play every musical instrument there was. He did make sure his children went regularly to the neighborhood school the few months each year it was taught. Mother started when she was five, old enough and strong enough to walk the two miles with Uncle Henry. Year after year she kept going, reading and re-reading McGuffey's sixth reader and memorizing poems such as "Thanatopsis," "The Village Blacksmith," and "Paul Revere's Ride."

Every year when the five months of school were over and she and Granddad were in the cornfield together again, he renewed his promise that she would certainly go to high school—if not this year, next year. Uncle Henry, after some blow-up with Granddad, went off to work on a river boat and then to the Navy. The other girls stayed at the house with Grandmother, especially when there was a little sister Evie, crippled with what they later thought was rheumatoid arthritis. When Mother was fourteen, another baby, Anna, was born. Grandmother missed Mother's good work in the house and the help with Evie but she would always say, "You go on to the field with Charley, Mary. He needs your company as much as your work." (Mother knew that he needed her work, too. He "depended" on her.)

The plan was that when Mother was eighteen she would go to board with relatives in Ohio County and attend the private academy, Hartford College, where one of Granddad's cousins was superintendent.

She was all those years and a month late entering high school. The last month was because she kept putting off leaving crippled Aunt Evie, from Sunday to Sunday until four Sundays had gone by. Then, driving with Granddad in the buggy behind the mules on the trip that took from early morning until night, she cried until noon. The next year when Granddad drove Mother to Hartford, Aunt Evie was dead, and Aunt Edna, the sister next to Mother in age, came along to enter school, too.

At the close of her first year, before Granddad came for her, she attended her first high-school graduation ceremony. There she saw the most beautiful young woman in the senior class, not one of the stiff-collared young men, walk out on the stage before the whole crowd and receive two gold medals, one for being the best Latin scholar that year and the other for having the best grade average in the graduating class. Two years later when Mother graduated from high school early because she received some credit for her work at home, she stood in that very spot and received the austere golden disc obviously designed for a male valedictorian, and the smaller stylized sun for the Latin scholar.

Mother's stories came out with the rhythm of work to be done, much as Granddad's talk with her had. I learned most of what I know of her history while picking blackberries or stringing beans or folding and sprinkling clothes to be ironed. With his and Mother's move from Texas to Kentucky, Daddy's stories took us into a world we did not remember seeing and held our complete attention. He wrapped his arms around his right knee pulled up on the chair he sat in, and narrowed his eyes at the corners, as he glimpsed the Texas of his childhood and youth. Grandfather Miller, Grandmother Susie, the six boys, and two girls became the figures in an epic, and the journeys back and forth across Texas in the covered wagon were the plot of the epic. When Grandfather Miller came into the story, I saw him as Abraham Lincoln and never knew until I was grown that he was not much taller than Daddy's five-feet-six. About the same time I found out that Grandma Susie was not the fabulously small Thumbelina that I had imagined, but a normal-sized woman crippled by a broken hip that was never set.

Daddy's Canaan, beautiful as it was, did not flow with milk and honey. We often heard about the five years without rain when the family lived on pinto beans. In the middle sixties at a hotel in London, Aunt Pearle, the sister who was closest to Daddy, told me that one of their trips was to take up residence on land in the Panhandle of Texas that Grandfather Miller bought for five dollars an acre. For five years he was not able to make a single payment on land later worth $1000 an acre after the deep wells were drilled; he gave it up and moved to Rule where Aunt Pearle and Daddy could go to high school.

Instead of being the responsible older child in the family like Mother, Daddy was the bright younger one indulged and loved by his older siblings, including Aunt Pearle, and looked up to by his younger brothers. We listened to the story of his first day in school over and over again. To start him off right, Grandfather Miller bought him a new pair of red high-top buttoned shoes. That first day he was promoted from the first grade to the third, because he had already learned to read and do arithmetic at home.

Daddy admitted that he had been first in his high school class although he did not brag about that honor as Mother did about hers. She liked bragging about him, too, and wanted us to know that we had a father whose marks through grade school and high school were solid blocks of 100s with only now and then a 96 or 98.

The two valedictorians met and fell in love while teaching in a little two-room school out on the plains of Texas. After high school and two or three years teaching in rural schools near home, and some terms at the University of Kentucky and the Bogue Institute for Stammerers in Indianapolis, Mother wanted to see the world, she told us. Her way of seeing it was to go out west to Texas. An uncle found a teaching position for her at Idella in Haskell County. My father who was demobilized from the army on December 21, 1918, after the November armistice, began teaching in January at the same school. They were married in March 1919.

Mother made vivid for us the January morning that Daddy joined her at Idella. He was still wearing his army uniform with the strap-around leather leggings. She was impressed that he removed his cavalry hat as he stepped in the side door at the front of the school room: "You would think that any teacher would know to take off his hat when he comes in the house, but they don't all do it, and I knew that he was a gentleman right away."

We have family pictures that show how they both looked then. Mother was proud of her fair, unblemished skin, always much complimented by her friends at the University of Kentucky, and her

beautiful hair, the great brown sheath of it, pushed up from her fore-
head and gathered on the back of her head. Her nose was straight,
her cheek bones high, and she carried herself well.

Daddy, born October 19, 1896, was four years younger and
only a few inches taller. He probably weighed twenty pounds less,
but his heavy dark eyebrows gave him a look of authority, and the
laugh lines around his eyes were deep even then. He had an Irish-
man's bulbous nose, big ears, and a full pointy mouth that he claimed
a cow-town dentist had ruined by pulling his overlapping eye teeth.
Having signed up for the cavalry because he liked horses, he had
spent most of the war taking care of flu patients in the army hospital
in San Antonio. He was as proud of having survived the great flu
epidemic as his son John was of having lived through the Battle of
the Bulge in World War II.

Mother had been on the verge of a decision to go back to
Kentucky and marry the school superintendent she had continued
to correspond with when Daddy turned up. She consented to marry
him only after he made two promises: that she would never have to
live on a farm and that he would not stand in the way of her becoming a minister. Mother did not want to live on a farm because "there
was too much work to it," hard physical labor of the kind she was
capable of but did not want to spend her life doing. We heard about
the second promise only years later when she told us she had decided
that she wanted to become a minister after hearing Mrs. Louisa M.
Woosley preach at her home church in the Little Bend.

Daddy had no trouble with the first promise. After a lifetime
of hard work, even with the help of six sons, Grandfather Miller had
died without owning his own farm. Daddy was as set against the
farm as Mother and, like her, delighted as much in the life of a student. They resigned their teaching positions at Idella when the term
was over and went to the University of Texas in Austin.

The bride and groom really did not have much but love in
their first weeks of marriage. They lived in a tent on the edge of the
land of the farmer with whose family Mother had been boarding and
drew water from his well. They slept on Daddy's army cot under his
army blanket, often gritty with sand. Mother did not often cry, but
when the tent collapsed under a heavy wind, she cried and asked

Daddy to make another promise: that she would never have to live in a tent again.

She was pregnant by the time they were ready to move. She had never expected that she would not be. When I asked her later about birth control, she said, "I never dreamed there could be such a thing, and I was so in love, I didn't care."

In Austin the two luxuriated in a rooming house, electric lights, running water, and a chance to study again. Both took part-time jobs, Mother teaching a room full of Mexican children. They assumed that a boy would be named "John Brison Miller, Jr.," but there was no agreement on a name for a girl. My father thought of himself as good at naming things. In the fall of 1916 he had received a five-dollar award for submitting "The Brand" as a name for the college newspaper at Simmons College (now Hardin-Simmons University) in Abilene, Texas, which he attended for a few terms. He announced on one of his early visits to the hospital after my birth, "I named the baby today."

Mother asked, "Well, darling, what did you name her?"

"I named her 'U.T.' for the University of Texas."

She always referred to Daddy in explaining how I got my name. "Her father called her 'U.T.' Yes, we always use the initials." She told me that she tried not to show her disappointment; it seemed like no name to her, but she knew that Daddy thought it would please her as a reflection of how far they had come.

Mother cried when Daddy made an investment in a popcorn machine which he hoped would take them through college. He planned to surprise her when he asked her to meet him on a busy corner where he was tending the machine: "What do you think, Sweetheart?" That was when the tears came: "I never thought to see my husband running a popcorn machine like an immigrant with a monkey." She had seen such a person when she was in Indianapolis.

They soon ran out of money. Everybody seems to have forgotten exactly why they moved to Marshall where my sister Mary Elizabeth was born. I know Daddy began selling maps. Mother was increasingly anxious to get back to Kentucky as she counted the years since she had seen Grandmother and Granddad. When a teacher's agency found them a job teaching together in Boston, Kentucky, they moved. None of us lived in Texas again until Mary Elizabeth went to live with Aunt Pearle for her last year of high school in 1938.

School Days, School Days

Both of my parents had a life-long romance with school. They liked the first they went to and the last—the little weather-beaten gray or white-washed country schools with the pump outside and the bell to ring in the children in the morning, high schools and academies of all sizes and types in towns of all sizes and kinds, teachers' colleges, denominational colleges, state universities. They also liked the great names like Yale, Harvard, Oxford, Cambridge.

They liked being pupils, students, scholars because they were good at it. And they liked being teachers because they were good at that, too.

Both liked chalk, blackboards, pencils, paper, ink, notebooks, rulers, compasses.

Mother liked crayons, water colors, construction paper, printing sets, flash cards, song books, pitch pipes, dumbbells, lunch boxes, book bags.

Daddy liked globes, maps, graphs, basketballs and courts to use them on—indoors and out—baseballs and bats and baseball diamonds, bleachers and rolls of tickets, stages with curtains that pull back and forth, and makeup and cold cream to take it off.

They both liked books. Daddy liked them in sets—like encyclopedias or histories of wars and of states or the complete works of almost anybody. He read fast and when he got started, he liked to know that there was more to come. All over the South and Southwest, wherever he traveled and worked, book salesmen had been there before him, and he found sets of books, that, with the exception of the first one or two volumes, no one had ever turned the pages of.

For herself, Mother liked school books, books that represented progress from one grade level to the next, readers, spellers, geography books, books of rules of all kinds including books of games and etiquette books, books from which languages could be learned, and of course, the Bible. For us and for Daddy, she liked the vistas beyond the practical that libraries open up. She had many reasons for disliking the country and loving town, but one of them was libraries, not private libraries, but libraries open to the public. Whoever heard of a library in the country? Who hadn't heard of the Louisville Free Public Library? There, indeed, was "God's plenty." If she didn't have time to absorb it all, she hoped that her husband and four children would. We had the impression that each book read was truly treasure laid up in heaven. We could never lose it.

Mother was also sure that scholarship ought to be and would be rewarded. My father saw scholarship as one of many talents.

At Home in LeGrande

My first sight of my father that I remember is by the flame of a hastily lighted coal oil lamp. Mother's hand held the match, her breath blew it out, and then she fitted on the globe. But it was my father's shout even more than the light that broke the dark, his legs that leaped, and my sister Mary Elizabeth who cried. She had wet the bed again, his bed. When she awoke scared at night she often slid into my parents' bed, and sometimes Mother was too sleepy to settle her again in the cradle. This time Daddy snapped awake, peed on and angry. While he got into dry underwear, Mother stirred up the coals in the fireplace and draped the wet sheet and Daddy's and Mary Elizabeth's wet clothes over two or three straight-backed chairs in front of the fire.

The smell of my childhood is the odor of urine-wet bed-clothes drying on chairs in front of the fireplace. Yet in all my life I cannot remember feeling more secure, comfortable, and comforted than on those winter nights when we all dropped off to sleep at about the same time, Mother and Daddy in their bed, sometimes talking low about the events of the day or plans for the future, each child in her separate crib or cradle in the same room. Whatever needed to be dried and was drying was part of the comfortableness.

Soon after we moved to Kentucky, Daddy became principal of the two-year high school in LeGrande, another crossroads in central Kentucky. He was also the history and math teacher, basketball and baseball coach, and play director. Mother taught English, Latin (both first-year and Caesar), civics and art. Their combined salaries were two hundred dollars a month and "the teacherage" next door to the school where we lived. We were never again so secure financially or enjoyed more luxury with our usual austerity. Help was cheap, and we had a full-time Negro woman helper who slept on a cot in the kitchen.

Much of our way of life was explained by "that's the way we did it down on the farm." Every bed in the house had a feather bed as did every bed in my grandparents' house. The amenities of electricity and town water and sewage were lacking in both LeGrande and on the farm. But my parents also had different ideas from their parents about how they wanted things at home and how to bring up their children.

Mother believed that your relationship with people began with the names you called them. She insisted on calling the children at school by their "real" names and not their nicknames and that we use some title in addressing the women who worked for us, "Miss" with her given name for the younger black women and "Aunt" for the older black women: "Yes, Miss Ethel," "No, Aunt Harriet." My father always called servants by their first names as he had been brought up to do in Texas and as everyone we knew in Kentucky did. Mother said that the fact that people did it didn't make it right.

We all used the same outside privy, and inside, a chamber pot for the children and a slop jar for my mother and father. And we carried our water from the school pump. For Saturday afternoon and Saturday night baths we heated water on the kitchen stove in a galvanized tin wash tub. Year round the weekly wash was done outside with a big iron pot to boil the water in and then the clothes. While the helper was getting breakfast ready, Mother began the process of boiling everything in the pot, sometimes with the rain or snow spitting in the fire and in her face. After the laundry was washed, it was hung on the line—in winter to freeze and partly dry.

Besides single beds ("When you have a bunch of kids piled up in the same bed, anything can happen"), we always said that our mother emphasized three other requirements for raising children: a yard fence, a cow, and a piano. In LeGrande we had no piano because Mary Elizabeth and I were still too little to take piano lessons, but we did have the yard fence and the cow. The fence was the same ordinary farm wire Grandmother and Granddad used around their larger yard to separate the family's living area from the lots for the farm animals. Our fence kept us children in, others out, and gave us an area for play where little supervision was needed.

On the other hand, Mother considered that the road where there was so little traffic once the students were at school was safe enough. Her father had kept his children too close to home except when they went to school or church. Mary Elizabeth was three and

I was five when we were allowed to hold hands and walk along the side of the road to the country grocery store. After our cow got into wild green onions, Mary Elizabeth insisted on smelling the store butter for which Mother had sent us.

As Mother wound up with much of the care of the cow, it was she who insisted on planting such a large garden that she had most of the care for it. My father was happy eating beans and bread and milk; Mother's ideal was the plenitude of her father's farm. Feeding herself and others, particularly the members of her own family, was a major pleasure in Mother's life. In times of anxiety or trouble, she would often say, "Well, let's have a little something to eat and we'll see how things are then." There was also her deep strain of prudence. The fable of the ant that provided for winter and the grasshopper that played around all summer had touched her almost as deeply as any Bible story, and we knew well that she belonged to the tribe of "ants."

At school Mother liked to have things looking pretty and that was where the art classes and art materials came in. She and the students made brown wrapping-paper shades with crayoned designs for both classrooms of the school. She also kept her students busy decorating for the different religious and public holidays which she felt had been skimped in her own upbringing: "We never paid much attention to those things at home, one day was pretty much like another."

Never remembering having celebrated a birthday at home, Mother made our birthdays almost as exciting as Christmas. It began when she was preparing Mary Elizabeth and me for the next baby, Caroline. She had heard the shocking physiological details of conception and birth on the playground at school, and when we were old enough to understand, she aimed to tell us the facts straight. Before we were six, she told us the romantic story that "the stork" brought babies. She showed us the picture in her German reader, and it was the stork that brought each of us a diaper of presents, tied to the head of our beds on any child's birthday: an orange, an apple, some raisins, and candy; and in later years, for us girls, a length of dress material.

Mother was pregnant most of her and Daddy's first year in LeGrande. Caroline was born on an April weekend; we saw her for the first time lying on a diaper in the lap of Aunt Harriet. Mother missed few, if any, days at school for Caroline's birth. Afterwards she nursed the new baby at times that fit in with her school schedule.

Along with the stork and the ant and the grasshopper, Mary Elizabeth and I became well acquainted with the Bible characters we heard about at the Methodist Sunday School up on the main road which we regularly attended Sunday afternoons. We always brought home small cards with brightly colored illustrations on one side and the stories that went with them on the other. Later in the week Mother sat down with us and the cards and talked about the stories. Moses, David, Daniel, Jesus were as real to us as relatives we had never seen but knew by their photographs.

An early theological lesson came in Mother's answer to a teenage helper who told us Mary Elizabeth would go to hell when she sneaked some cookies from a cookie jar and refused to admit it. I did not want my sister to go to hell and to her disgust gave away her secret to the baby-sitter by crying. When Mother was told, as she had to be, she promised that nobody but God could say who would go to hell.

Mother and Daddy were lucky to be in a community which was very proud of its school and worked hard for its growth. Mr. F. M. Richardson, whose family I remember as our friends in Le-Grande, had led his neighbors in building the first one-room school which opened with twenty-five pupils in 1915. By the time my parents arrived in 1923 there was a two-room two-year high school with a teacherage and an enrollment of ninety.

Mother and Daddy aimed to make History and Latin as important to their rural students as the subjects were to them. But our father's dramatic productions and ball games were equally useful in maintaining high community spirit and an enrollment well beyond the seventy-five students required by state law to keep a school open.

In the plays Daddy usually gave himself whatever role required the most skill to make people laugh. He liked to disguise himself in the whiskers of an old farmer or the black face of a Negro. Once as a Chinaman in pajamas and queue rented from a costume house in Louisville he put out a fire on stage caused by a lit cigarette dropped into a waste basket by the play's villain. The audience thought his dash, pig-tail flying, to the rain barrel behind the school was part of the play.

He was also good at keeping order both at school and on public occasions. The belt he wore, not suspenders like less athletic and older businessmen, not overalls like farmers, was his policeman's billy and revolver. He also had plenty of jokes and wisecracks that helped make people laugh instead of fight and a reliable sense of who might start trouble. Mother liked to hear from friends and neighbors how well her husband handled any altercation.

The need to transport his ball players back and forth when they played other schools, and the heavy schedule he was very soon into, influenced him to buy his first car. He also looked forward to getting out on the road and selling maps during school vacations. Mother expressed emphatically and often her dislike of that first machine. She never liked any of the later ones either and dated our financial troubles from the moment of his first car purchase. We children were always eager to go anywhere and were sympathetic with our father. The car seemed to back up Mother. Like a balky mule, it did everything possible to embarrass Daddy: refused to start, boiled over, got stuck in the mud, inevitably blew its tires, sometimes two or three times on one trip.

Our mother was probably right about the expense of the car. Not only did the car consume gas, batteries, and tires, but it took us to places where there were desirable things to buy. At the furniture store in Horse Cave, we bought the only "new furniture" we were ever to own: a glassed-in bookcase, a vanity dresser for Mother, and the pretty pink crib for Mary Elizabeth when Caroline went from bassinet to cradle. Another expense was family photographs made in Mumfordville. Thrifty as they were in many ways, Mother and Daddy were in the habit of spending most of the money they made every month.

No savings did not mean that they were not thinking about the future, however. Familiar as any lullaby was the murmur of their voices when we were all in bed at night that second year in Le-Grande. They seemed to have much to talk about. "Our degrees," "credits," "registration," "Bowling Green" were words that floated up and hung in the air when we were just about to drop off to sleep.

First, Mother's voice, "With your college work in Texas, and mine in Kentucky and Texas, it wouldn't take more than a year or so for us to get our degrees."

Then Daddy's, "Whoever heard of anybody going to school with three children?"

"Why, darling, we could go with four, even five." Our father shuddered.

"If we want to make a living teaching school, we need our degrees," said Mother.

"Teaching school is no way to make what I call a living."

As well as we were getting along and as much as he liked teaching and enjoyed his position in the community, he was not making the living that would impress the people who had expected him to do so well.

Mother kept up her bedtime pleading, "With our degrees we will do a lot better even if we don't get rich. Besides I don't want to die without being able to say that I have a college education. I want my children's father to have a college education, too." Eventually Daddy agreed to Mother's urging and with Granddad's name on the note, she was able to come up with the $1,000 from Cousin Wash Brown that was supposed to see them through their degrees at Western Kentucky State Teachers' College in Bowling Green.

The Farm and the Church

We expected Mother to cry when she heard certain songs, especially "Home Sweet Home" or "My Old Kentucky Home" or "The Little Brown Church in the Wildwood." "Home Sweet Home" was my grandfather's farm in the Little Bend of the Green River in western Kentucky. "The Little Brown Church" was actually white, about a mile and a half from the farm.

Mother's yearning for home was the main reason she and Daddy moved from Texas to Kentucky. Wherever we lived during the decade we were in the state, we always came back to the Little Bend in the summer and sometimes at Christmas. When we lived in Bowling Green, we came and went a few times by river boat. From the other six villages and towns we lived in during those years, we crisscrossed the state by train and bus, waiting for hours at places like Russellville and Central City. Sometimes Daddy drove us, rarely staying longer than overnight because he was always anxious to get back on the road selling maps in the first years, and insurance later.

My mother's youngest sister whom we called "Anna," rather than "Aunt Anna," documented one of our first visits with her Kodak: me sticking my head out of one of those old-fashioned valises Anna had popped me into, Mary Elizabeth and me in white caps and white stockings standing on the farmhouse porch holding hands and squinting into the sun.

We never approached the farm from whatever direction by whatever means of conveyance without a flip-flop of happiness as we came to the last landmarks: the mailbox that marked the lane to the house, the opening in the trees that was the boat landing.

A part of our joy was the knowledge that these were what Mother called "our people." We knew we were being waited for. If we were coming by car, and probably most often we were, somebody was listening for the motor and the opening and closing of the gate at the bottom of the hill. Grandmother would be outside the yard gate before we pulled in front of the barn. Granddad would wait in his rocker on the porch until he was really sure it was us. Dawn-to-dark worker that he prided himself on being, he did not go far from the house during the hours of our possible arrival. We were out of the car in a great burst. Grandmother, her glasses misting up, first kissed Mother, who was trying to keep from crying. Mother passed whoever was the baby to Grandmother. Grandmother held the baby out from her, gave it an approving look from head to toe, and passed it back to Mother or to Anna or whatever other woman was present, then stooped and kissed each of the rest of us children. Granddad with his big stomach did not find it easy to bend over enough to submit to being kissed, and we always had to stand on tiptoe.

We entered the white clapboarded house by the porch which extended halfway across the front and the length of the side of the house. In the living room at the front were Grandmother's and Granddad's double beds with the high old-fashioned headboards. If we were the only visitors we usually took over "the Girls' Room" with another pair of high head-boarded double beds and a fireplace that could be lit in winter. Successively the babies slept in the big low wooden cradle that Aunt Evie slept in until she died.

Unless we were too late, Grandmother would save the chicken eggs to gather with the children. Every child who could walk followed at her heels as she went to the hen house, the cow barn, the horse barn, up ladders while she warned us to stay below. I don't remember that any eggs were ever broken. With her little hickory-split basket, she knew just how to handle both children and eggs, holding out her water-softened, arthritic-knuckled hand to receive the occasional warm egg one of us was so proud of finding.

Except in the coldest winter weather when the cows stayed in the barn, Granddad or Anna had to herd them down the hill and past the woods to the distant pasture where they spent their days, and drive them back at night. It was fun to go with Anna after we were old enough to walk so far. Sometimes Mary Elizabeth went with Granddad who otherwise set off alone with his stick and his dog. He thought cows didn't like children and he didn't like fooling with children himself, except for a few favorites like Anna when she was little and Mary Elizabeth who was the first baby he knew in our family.

They did not have electricity until the very last years they lived at the farm, after Roosevelt's Rural Electrification program had reached that part of the country, so they did not have milking machines. The sale of cream, however, skimmed by the hand-turned cream separator in the kitchen and regularly collected by a company truck, was an important part of farm income. That meant eight or ten, or sometimes more, cows to milk by hand, night and morning. Even when Granddad had a hired man, which was by no means all the time, one of the women usually helped—Grandmother if nobody else was there, Mother or Anna when they were at home. Daddy, a farm boy himself, milked a few times, but after his day of driving he was usually urged to sit in a rocking chair and read the *Courier-Journal* or the *Saturday Evening Post* which Granddad would enjoy talking about later.

The house was on a little rise and from the side porch you could look out on the farm land. There were about two hundred acres of pastures, woods on the hills, and cropland which included bottom land, so good for corn, that ended in a fringe of trees along Green River. The big horse barn was the first thing you saw when you came up the hill from the lane that led to the mail box; you could also see what was called the "cow barn" from the porch. Beside and behind the house was the chicken lot with the chicken house and the other farm outbuildings. At the very back was the two-hole privy where cousins spent many companionable hours looking at the mail order catalogues that were also used for toilet paper.

There were fences and gates everywhere to mark the different uses of the land and to keep the animals in their places. The exception was the chickens, few of which stayed in the chicken yard. Though we thought of the chickens as Grandmother's, the choice of white Leghorns instead of Domineckers or Rhode Island Reds was Granddad's, not only because they laid well, but because he liked the look of the white dots spread out over the farm.

In the attic off the Girls' Room we found Anna's old doll and doll-buggy to play with. "What I wouldn't have given for a doll and carriage like that," Mother sometimes sighed when she looked at the high-wheeled leatherette stroller and the doll with real hair and open-and-shut eyes. (She could never quite forgive Anna for having been born after the farm began to prosper, and for being able to go to high school in Beaver Dam at fourteen instead of eighteen.) The spinning wheel, on which Grandmother had spun the wool for winter blankets in the days when Granddad kept sheep, was also in the attic, as was the attic trunk with treasures of old dresses and underwear that Mother and Grandmother could remember who wore and when.

Anna was the first "grown girl" Mary Elizabeth and I knew, and more than anything we liked to watch her primp. In the summer she could see better to pluck her eyebrows on the front porch than in the daytime darkened house, and the two of us sat as close as we could on each side of her to look with her into the mirror she held in her hand. We squeezed almost as close in winter when she lit the kerosene lamp on the dresser in the "front room" and thrust the curling iron down the chimney before twisting her red-brown hair between the blades. The smell of slightly burned hair was a part of the thrill of watching her get ready for the young men Mother and Grandmother called her "beaux," and she and her girlfriend Miss Evie (the same name as our dead aunt's) called their "boyfriends."

Many Sunday afternoons Anna and Miss Evie entertained the young men in "Anna's Room." The parlor had been known as that since our aunt began to have boyfriends. The room smelled of the imitation black leather davenport, overstuffed rocker, and club chair which Granddad must have bought during one of the war years when the crops were doing well. There was also a floor-model "Victrola" run by a handle on the side. Mother's own framed diploma from Hartford College hung for many years over the mantel above the fireplace. On the two sides of the mantel were the small matching urns with roses painted inside gold medallions that Aunt Edna, the daughter who died of a tumor, gave to Grandmother after President Wilson declared the second Sunday in May "Mother's Day." On the wall hung Aunt Edna's graduation picture in brown sepia, all soft white tulle around her neck and shoulders and soft brown hair piled on her head. Grandmother and Mother tried to keep Mary Elizabeth and me at the back of the house when Anna was entertaining, but more than once we managed to sneak out and stand in the bed of day lilies under the parlor windows and listen to records like "The Little Rosewood Casket" and "The Baggage Coach Ahead." While they listened to those sad pieces, the young people ate fudge and coconut fondant candy and drank lemonade made from well water. I can still see Anna's and Miss Evie's legs in their silk stockings, the dips and swirls of their chiffon dresses, and the yellowish pattern the rusty screen made on Mary Elizabeth's and my noses and foreheads as we leaned against it.

After the girls came back from college, the songs would be livelier, "Yes sir, that's my baby. No sir, I don't mean maybe."

It was from Anna and Miss Evie that Mary Elizabeth and I got our idea for the game, "Grown Girl," which required us to dress up in clothes Mother, Anna, and Grandmother handed down to us and to go on dates with pretend boys. Since we both liked to dress up, neither of us ever wanted to be a boy.

"The Little Brown Church," actually white, was the Point Pleasant Cumberland Presbyterian Church in a grove of oak and hickory trees—from my grandparents' farm a mile and a half by the road and a little less distant across the pastures and through the woods. This was the church where Mother was baptized and where she heard Mrs. Louisa Woosley preach. Mrs. Woosley was the first woman minister Mother ever saw.

Why the family had always gone to Point Pleasant never seemed to require explanation. The fact that it was "not Baptist" like the only other church in the neighborhood, the one much nearer to the farm up on the hill beyond Granddad's woods, and that nobody in the family had ever been Baptist, was reason enough.

I can remember going with Granddad to Point Pleasant in both the wagon and the seldom used "surrey," the two-seated buggy which still stood in the barn. But usually we went in the mule-drawn wagon. If any other man went, he sat in the wagon seat with Granddad, but usually it was Mary Elizabeth after she was big enough to sit up without falling. Grandmother and Mother and any other women sat in chairs behind them, holding whoever was the baby and carrying parasols to shade them from the sun. The rest of the children sat on a quilt in the wagon bed, trying not to get our feet on each others' Sunday clothes and complaining if anybody did. The church was much like the one at LeGrande, except that the grounds with all the trees were prettier. The one large room was white clapboard on the outside and sealed on the inside with plain varnished planks. Kerosene lamps went up and down on pulleys so they could be lit for services in the evening. Pot-bellied stoves on each side of the church, with pipes wired to the high ceiling and walls, heated it in the winter. A bucket of water with a dipper stood on the platform a few feet from the pulpit. One of the old-fashioned hand pumped country organs accompanied the hymn singing.

Mother was always proud that Granddad had helped to build the church in 1904, hauled lumber, and although "a big man like him had no business on ladders," actually worked with hammer and nails. Granddad had professed religion when he was in his teens and an aunt spoke to him at a revival and propelled him by the elbow up to the altar. On preaching Sundays, he usually went into church and sat in the back rows. He was never asked and never volunteered for public prayers. He did ask the blessing in his own home if there wasn't a preacher present or if Mother had not suggested that he call on one of us.

Not just preaching, but Sunday school meant a great deal to Grandmother. She studied her Sunday school lesson every week, and took almost the whole month to read her church paper, "The Cumberland Presbyterian." She never taught Sunday school and I don't think she had much to say in class but "liked to hear the others talk." From early spring until late fall, she walked the back way across the farm to the church yard about once a week and changed the water and replaced the flowers in the mason jars set down into the graves of Aunt Evie and Aunt Edna, and later, Uncle Henry. It was the graves she had particularly in mind when she planted the zinnias and marigolds along the fence in front of the house and in the vegetable garden. She also put flowers on the grave of a neighborhood girl, said to be pregnant, who drowned herself in Green River.

We were given very special treatment on those Sundays at

Point Pleasant. After church services were over, our progress from the church door to the wagon to go home was one long embrace for Mother in which we all shared: "Kiss so and so," "Kiss so and so," as Mother tried to explain where each person fit into her life before we were born. The older farmers and their wives called her "Mary," and her former pupils in at least two local schools before she went to Texas called her "Miss Mary."

Usually, when everybody had been spoken to, we went behind the church to the graveyard where Aunt Evie and Aunt Edna were buried. Aunt Evie's tombstone was the shorter of the two thin shafts in the family plot. I always associated her with Beth in *Little Women*: sweet-looking, intelligent, with gray eyes and light brown braids. Many years later I heard from an acquaintance that she cried a lot, something nobody in the family ever admitted, though we knew that she was often in pain. Everybody was always on the lookout for something to please her: new kittens, baby chicks, a pretty wild flower. Granddad carried her in his arms to look at the calves and the lambs, and whenever he could, brought her the water from a special spring.

It was right that Aunt Edna's shaft in the cemetery was a little taller than Evie's as she was the young lady and Evie was the child. Mother loved Edna more than anyone in the world and always said that she was "perfectly beautiful." Besides her tombstone, we had her graduation picture to tell us what she looked like, as well as the Mother's Day vases, and "Aunt Edna's tree," a cedar tree she had brought in from the woods and planted by the front step of the porch. The summer after she graduated from Hartford College, Granddad paid $100 to two specialists to come from Louisville to examine the tumor in her side and draw off the water that had accumulated. The tumor had gone too far, though, and she died before the summer was over.

In all those towns and villages where we moved, anyone who seemed likely to become our friend heard the stories of the family deaths. Mother blamed Aunt Evie's and Aunt Edna's on the country medicine, and that made her all the more determined to raise her children where there were hospitals and properly trained doctors.

While we were in the cemetery, if there wasn't Dinner-on-the-Ground at the church, Granddad would be out in the church yard, asking about half the congregation home to dinner, knowing Grandmother or Anna had made a cake and pies the day before. We were hardly in the house before Grandmother had changed her Sunday dress and was out in the yard wringing the necks of several chickens. Granddad was off to the garden to gather an armload of fresh corn for roasting. It wouldn't take long for Grandmother and Mother and the aunts to fry up the chickens, roll out some biscuits and make some corn bread. Somebody shelled the butterbeans that had been gathered the day before. Granddad usually invited families with children and there were often two families of aunts, uncles, and cousins: Mother's older brother Uncle Henry with Aunt Barbara and J. G. and Dorcas, and her younger sister, Aunt Allye with Uncle Robert and Lucille and Conrad. Somebody was likely to bring ice to make ice cream in the home freezer that was always a part of the kitchen equipment.

In later years Mother claimed to hate the big Sunday dinners for which she saw Granddad getting all the glory and Grandmother and the daughters all the work. We loved the Sunday dinners for both the glory and the company. And the fact is that Mother enjoyed the company as much as anyone; she worked hard to make every dinner a grand occasion. She also enjoyed the prestige Granddad enjoyed in the community. He had the reputation of "setting the best table" in the Little Bend. Never mind that it was his women who actually cooked the food and cleaned up afterward.

Mother and we children went to the farm expecting to stay somewhere between several days and a month. Daddy rarely stayed longer than overnight, and I don't remember his being present for more than one or two of those Sunday dinners. The family, however, respected his need to get back on the road selling.

The Love of Cities

Both my parents loved cities as they loved schools. Daddy enjoyed them for the spectacle, the color, and the possibility of the unexpected. Temperamentally he was suited to the city's combination of solitude and companionship.

Mother not only enjoyed towns and cities; she believed deeply in the superiority of city life to country life. She associated the city with health, safety, and education; the country, with ignorance, disease, and filth of many kinds. Evil was perpetrated in barns and in the woods. Education, good manners, good clothes, a refined way of talking were all a part of the city. When you found these characteristics in the country, somebody had worked against odds to achieve them. If she ever heard of "white collar crime," she would not have called it that. One of the things she liked most about the city was seeing men wearing suits and collars and ties instead of overalls. She liked to see their faces shaved and their hair cut. I now realize how closely my father, country-born and bred, conformed to this ideal of hers. One seldom saw him in a pair of overalls, and with his speech training and good vocabulary he talked like a city man, even using the newspaper slang of the comics and the sports pages.

Mother took an almost sensual pleasure in paved streets, sidewalks, and street lights. She always remembered Aunt Edna's first night in Hartford when she pointed to a street light and said, "Oh, Mary, what's that thing that looks like a goose egg." Mother was saddened, "I felt so sorry that the little thing had had so few advantages."

Bowling Green

On the walls of a room in the teacherage at LeGrande hung one of the big wall maps of Kentucky that Daddy sold during the summers. I learned to read from studying it when everybody else was asleep or busy and then asking questions when somebody had time to pay attention to me. The smaller the dot, the smaller the settlement or crossroads. LeGrande was very small indeed. A circle around the dot meant that Morgantown was the county seat of Butler County where my grandparents lived. Bowling Green was not as big as Louisville and Lexington, nor as large as cities not on the map like Amarillo and San Antonio (Daddy's Rome and Paris), nor Indianapolis, Mother's example of "a real city," but it was much larger than either LeGrande or Horse Cave. With a population of about 12,000 in 1926, it was the largest town the family was ever to live in, with many of the "advantages" that Mother associated with the city.

The road in front of our house in Forest Park on the western edge of Bowling Green was not paved, and our frame house was much like the one in LeGrande, with coal-burning fireplaces for heat and a wood-burning stove for cooking. We still had a privy behind the house, our dung-splashed cow behind her own fence, and the front yard fence for us children. The big differences from LeGrande were the running water from a faucet in the kitchen instead of an outdoor pump, and light, not from kerosene lamps, but from bulbs that hung from the ceilings and turned on with wall switches. Again we had a $5-a-week helper, a very large white woman, "Miss Pearl," who slept in the kitchen.

Western Kentucky State Teachers' College, now Western Kentucky University, was on top of the highest hill in the area. No college or university I saw in later years ever seemed so grand to me. Daddy, Mother, Mary Elizabeth, and I became well acquainted with that hill and the view from it, as we walked from Forest Park every school day. Daddy had sold the family car soon after he moved us from LeGrande, and Mother was pregnant again with our brother

John who would be born in November 1925.

Mother was thrilled that Mary Elizabeth and I could attend the kindergarten of the Training School at Western. Kindergarten was another of those magical privileges available only to a few lucky children who lived in towns like Bowling Green. Daddy would have been satisfied for us to go to kindergarten at the Model Rural School which was also part of the college's training program, and where my parents would not have had to pay $10-a-term tuition per child, but Mother said that she had had enough of rural schools. When a neighbor whose older children went to the Model School protested that four- and five-year-olds walking so far alone would be run over or kidnapped, Mother warned us against getting into cars with strangers. She insisted that she wanted her children to be independent.

Our first day of school Daddy, taking each of us by the hand, made the long walk with us, over the railroad track, past the football field and up the hill to the Training School. Miss Jones, our tall curly-haired kindergarten teacher, bent gracefully from the waist to shake our hands and tell us that she had been looking forward to having sisters in her class. Daddy did not have to wait five minutes to help us adjust to new surroundings. Back home that night he agreed that Miss Jones was pretty and said that she was also known as the best kindergarten teacher in Kentucky. He never complained again about our going to the Training School although after the first day we were expected to walk alone.

Going to a "real Sunday School" was another opportunity that Mother aimed for us not to miss. The somewhat old-fashioned building of the Cumberland Presbyterian Church was on a side street. In contrast, both the brick First Christian Church and the white limestone First Presbyterian, each with Greek columns, were on a main street. During our first months in Bowling Green Daddy started Mary Elizabeth and me going to Sunday school at the First Christian Church. In the spring when he managed to juggle his college schedule so that he could buy another car and go on the road selling insurance again, Mother started us going to her church, the First Presbyterian. Besides being a Presbyterian, she was looking forward to infant baptism for Caroline and John which the Presbyterian Church practiced and the Christian Church did not.

Mary Elizabeth and I were more faithful churchgoers than either of our busy parents and happily went to both churches. Some people objected to the waste of money for those fancy Sunday school papers and picture cut-outs given by more wealthy Sunday schools. They were wrong, as far as we were concerned. The handouts from the two churches were equally beautiful, and we faithfully took them home, retold the stories to Mother, and tied them together with ribbons to make books. Mother marveled at how much more "up-to-date" the city Sunday Schools were than anything she had known as a child.

Even with the hospital in town, our brother was born at home. We three girls were sleeping in our back bedroom then, and our parents slept in one of the two front rooms. The morning after the baby was born Daddy came in to start Mary Elizabeth and me dressing for school. He didn't tell us anything until Mary Elizabeth said:

"I heard a baby crying last night."

"Yes, after you were in bed Dr. Honekker came and brought us a baby boy. He and Mother are sleeping now and you can't see them before you go to school, but I think they will be ready for a visit tonight."

Back home in the evening, Miss Pearl gave us our supper as usual in the kitchen and took Mother's supper to her on a tray. After Daddy had washed Caroline's hands and face and dressed her in her sleeping clothes, he took her in his arms, and we all visited Mother and the baby. Mary Elizabeth and I tiptoed across the floor and kissed Mother on the cheek. She was wearing a clean white nightgown, her hair over her shoulder in one neat braid as she wore it at night before she had it cut, and her tired eyes smiling. The tiny little red baby was tucked under the cover between her and the wall. Daddy lifted Caroline up across the bed so that she could see the baby, too. We tiptoed out of the room. Daddy tucked us in our beds with kisses on our cheeks like the kisses we had given Mother.

About Christmas time we received our first report cards in kindergarten. My high marks were in "application" and "manners"; Mary Elizabeth's were in "initiative," "leadership," and "friendliness." Long after we had left Bowling Green, Mother kept repeating the defining words to explain to people in each new town just what the different strong points of the two of us were. At mid-term I was promoted to first grade since I had learned to read before I came to school. My first grade teacher Miss Lee, with her short straight hair and her less stylish clothes, began to seem as pretty as Miss Jones when my report card was a solid block of E's for "excellent." All the qualities of character were compressed into the single category "conduct" and the other marks were for reading, writing, and arithmetic, so I was promoted to the second grade after half a year.

Mother was sure that Mary Elizabeth and I were as good at our books as we proved to be because we started school at the Teachers' College Training School. (Mary Elizabeth wasn't that poor in "application.") Mother ignored the fact that in later life Caroline did just as well as Mary Elizabeth and I, although she cried so hard when Daddy tried several times to drop her off at kindergarten that she never attended the Training School a single day.

In every way, the Training School offered the broadening of horizons that Mother had in mind when Mary Elizabeth and I were sent there. John Dewey's ideas about learning by doing had clearly reached the Kentucky Teachers' College by then. In second grade my class read Longfellow's "Hiawatha," decorated burlap bags with colored chalk to make Indian blankets, and built an Indian village in a sand box. At rest period our teachers read us books like *Doctor Doolittle*, *Raggedy Ann*, and many fairy stories that children in schools we went to later had never heard of.

Just as important as our class work was the background of most of our classmates. With a sprinkling of pupils from other Teachers' College student families, most of them were the children of the more affluent town families: the faculty members of the college, the doctors, the president of the downtown Business College, and the more prosperous and enlightened business people. The most enviable children in any class were those who gave everybody a valentine on Valentine's Day and invited everybody in the class to their birthday parties. Whenever either Mary Elizabeth or I received such an invitation, Mother called from a neighbor's phone and asked if we could both come so the one invited wouldn't have to walk home alone after the party. As it turned out, some generous parent always offered to take us home, and Mary Elizabeth and I went to about twice as many birthday parties as any other children of college students. Together we saw inside several houses much grander than any we had ever seen before, houses with chandeliers, matching suites of furniture, elaborately arranged drapes in beautiful materials, kitchens with built-in kitchen cabinets, refrigerators, and stoves heated by electricity or gas. Everybody had a telephone. No one had a cow, a privy, or a vegetable garden.

Church also increased our knowledge of the difference in the way "nice people" lived. When Mother or Daddy was not with us, we walked as many different ways as we could figure out, usually choosing the streets with the fine big houses. As we got farther from Forest Park we walked more slowly, discussing with each other our likes and dislikes in building materials, architectural details, and planting. When the curtains were open we could sometimes see the people inside and delighted in the domestic life of the well-off who, like our mother and father sometimes, did not go to church on Sunday morning. We saw their silver coffee pots, dignified dressing gowns, the backs of Sunday papers. The well-off who went to church, and especially their wives, were interesting, too. Whenever I looked up from crayoning Noah or Daniel in one Sunday School class, I met the glance of the topaz-eyed fox encircling the neck of the teacher.

Mother who thought so much about how we ought to be brought up was also influenced by her courses in "Child Development" and "Child Nutrition" as well as by the children's books she and I began to bring home from the college library. I had my first birthday cake with candles on my sixth birthday. We colored Easter eggs our first Easter in Bowling Green, and had our first Easter baskets. Mother pointed out to Daddy how right they had been to bring the cow to Bowling Green so each of their children could have a quart of milk a day. We usually ate half an orange for breakfast and ate prunes in multiples of four for the correct number of milligrams of iron. She put the same emphasis she always had on baths, the regular one bath a week, although the books called for two, and it hurt her that in our home that was not practical. The books also made her more strict about a bowel movement every day. When she

45

asked if we were constipated, I can't remember ever saying "yes." It seemed too monstrous a thing to admit to.

Early in the year that I was in second grade, Mother's sister, Anna, came for her first term at the Teachers' College. She had just finished teaching her first country school in a remote part of Butler County after passing the examination for her teacher's certificate. Uncle Henry who had driven her there at the beginning of the country school year had phoned Granddad to come take her home after he had seen the log house she would have to live in and some of the big old rough boys she would have to handle. Granddad, however, instead of making it easy for her, as Mother always claimed he did, said she ought to find out what life was like and what she was made of. She held her own with the boys and weathered part of the winter in the log house, even when the snow came through the chinks in the bedroom wall. But she was ready for another kind of life when she came to live in Bowling Green in a boarding house near the college with Miss Evie and another friend from high school.

Mary Elizabeth and I were dropped off to stay with them once or twice on Sunday afternoons when Mother and Daddy went to some special occasion at the college. Being with Anna and Miss Evie again was like a continuation of the story game "Grown Girl" that we had first thought of after seeing them at Grandmother's. Supposed to be studying, they would set us down on a twin bed with their boxes of costume jewelry, hand mirrors, and photograph albums. We tried to be quiet, but sometimes they were the ones who forgot and went on talking about their boyfriends and their dates. We soon knew the names of all their boyfriends, so we didn't have to ask "Who's that?" except when somebody new appeared in the photograph albums. It seemed to us that their way of going to school was much better than that of our parents who had to work so hard when they were not studying.

We continued to hear the words of the academic bureaucracy which had come to us at night in LeGrande, and others were added, such as the titles of positions and offices: "president," "dean," "registrar," and "doctor" for teachers with certain kinds of degrees; the names of various branches of learning. Daddy helped a few friends with their "algebra." Mother had a second cousin in the "zoology" department. "Annual" was the name for the yearbook which showed pictures of our parents and their teachers and fellow students, and when we moved away, helped assure us that we had really lived in Bowling Green.

The week of graduation, Mother made an appointment at the most expensive photography studio in Bowling Green for her and Daddy to have their pictures taken in their caps and gowns with the four children. Black-gowned, they held their heads stiffly to balance the caps; the bangs of the girls were freshly cut square across their foreheads; the baby, John B., sat in Mother's lap with large white feet sticking out of his dress. All the relatives received copies and whenever a new friend entered our house afterward, Mother brought out the picture.

Mother had been sure that at the last minute she would be able to persuade Grandmother and Granddad to come to the Commencement. There were several friends and neighbors with automobiles who could drive them the forty miles from the Little Bend to Bowling Green in good weather. But Granddad said, "You'll never get me in one of those machines, not until I can't help myself." He would live long enough to be less adamant about automobiles. Meanwhile he stayed close enough to home for the mules, old Jude and old Beck, to make it back to the barn at night. I can remember Grandmother standing on the steps of the Administration Building at Western with the sun glinting off her gold-rimmed glasses as the graduates passed. We were all thrilled. The farthest we had ever seen her away from home was Uncle Henry's store on one side of the farm and the church on the other. It was almost as though our grandmother couldn't exist anywhere but in the crook of the river and yet here she was.

Traveling by Riverboat

The summer after Mother and Daddy graduated from college we took our first trip by river boat to Grandmother and Granddad's.

In the lucky period of the middle and late '20s mail was still delivered by river packet in the Green River Valley, and there was regular passenger service from Bowling Green to Evansville, Indiana. You heard the boat whistle and saw the smokestacks and splashing paddle wheel among the riverside trees from the side porch of my grandparents' house. The boats accommodatingly stopped at any farm along the river to let passengers, farm freight and animals off and on.

Daddy cared almost as much about new experiences for us children as Mother cared about good nutrition and Sunday School. After graduation in 1926 he was also eager to get back on the road selling insurance. That summer and the next it was he who insisted that Mother and we children take the day and a half trip by riverboat from Bowling Green to Granddad's boat landing on the Green River.

On the days we left we could hear the boat whistle in the early morning darkness from our house in Forest Park and knew we needed to dress quickly. It was light when Daddy parked the Model T close to the edge of the river on the paved landing. He held Caroline's hand and Mother's arm as she carried baby John B. and they walked up the gangplank. Mary Elizabeth and I walked carefully behind them in the very middle of the gangplank to avoid falling into what we imagined was a bottomless river.

We used two cabins with upper and lower berths. At night the family separated, Mary Elizabeth on the upper berth in the cabin with Mother and John B. and Caroline in the lower berth in my cabin. During the day, Mary Elizabeth and I held hands and wandered over the entire boat. We spent as much time as we could in the women's rest room looking at the boat's paddle wheel through the open hole of the toilet seat. It was a dizzying distance down to the powerful blades which flung up sheets of white water, and yet the spray was almost close enough to sprinkle us.

On the first trip, one man and then another stood pretty little Mary Elizabeth on the deck rail and pointed out the sights to her. Quiet and older, I stood nearby, torn between envy at the attention she received and pride that she was my sister.

Both dinner and supper, served on big thick china plates, were like Grandmother's Sunday dinners; breakfast was like her company breakfasts. At night we settled down under the tightly pulled covers of the berths, felt the throbbing of the boat's engine and pictured the paddle wheel turning under the toilet. As it began to be daylight, the river mist slowly dissolved through my transom window and the trees along the river banks became more and more green.

We were ready to get off at many bends in the river before Granddad's landing. Mother, carrying John B. and holding Caroline's hand, thought she recognized this neighbor's bottom land and that one's landing long before it was time. The boat seemed to know where Granddad lived though, even if our mother didn't. It was moving in toward shore before we noticed the little figures who gradually became Grandmother and the hired man, Johnny Hawes. We proudly pointed them out to the friends we had made on the boat. Mother began to cry in a restrained way. Granddad was hanging onto the mules and the wagon at the top of the bank. One of the things that needed to be taken off the boat the first year was a rocking chair with the bark still on the wood for Granddad to use on the front porch. It was Mother's "thank-you for graduation" present to him. For Grandmother, a lap-sized glass churn with a wheel to turn to make butter was brought to replace the big crockery churn like the one we used as long as we had a cow. Grandmother used it for the rest of her life.

When we made the return trip to Bowling Green at the end of that first summer, the boat had to be signaled with a lantern at night. Grandmother had us spread "pallets" on a cleared space near the river bank some time before the boat was due, and everybody except Granddad and Mary Elizabeth lay down with mosquito netting over them. Granddad didn't trust anyone except himself to see the boat coming. Mary Elizabeth tagged along with him even though the mosquitoes were biting her legs.

As a matter of fact, it was Mary Elizabeth who saw the boat first. "That's it! That's it!" she shrilled into the dark. The thrashing of the paddle wheel and the appearance of more lights proved her right, and my Aunt Anna stood on the very edge of the river and swung the lantern. Granddad made a fuss about the boxes filled with half gallons of blackberries and peaches canned by Mother which had to be loaded on the boat. Granddad said, "Most foolish thing I ever heard of, carrying them all that way. You could have at least put enough sugar with them to make jam or jelly." When Daddy made the same complaint in Bowling Green about how heavy the boxes were to unload, Mother commented on men: "If you are really about to accomplish something, they will do everything they can to stop you."

The paddle-wheel steamer stopped running in the thirties. Sometimes I am envious of friends ten or twenty years younger, who will have that many more years to learn how our world will turn out. Then I remember two things: one is arriving at school in second grade in Bowling Green to hear that Lindbergh had flown the Atlantic; the other is those steamboat trips. If I had been born even ten years later, I would have missed both.

Country Relatives and Food

I associated the different relatives with the different foods we ate at their houses. Aunt Barbara, Uncle Henry's wife, tasted like the horehound candy that came out of the glass jars in their country store. She was nervous and creative and a talker. She embroidered, smocked, crocheted and talked constantly as she worked, never looking up except to receive a compliment. I don't think I ever heard her laugh, although her eyes occasionally brightened over those compliments.

My Aunt Allye was round-cheeked and round-armed like Mother. When we stopped by after six months or a year, she came out of the house wiping her round arms on her apron before she threw them around us, acting as though our growth were the most miraculous thing in the world, "Why did you ever?" Her flavor was the damsons and apricots that grew on her and Uncle Robert's farm and nowhere else I knew about.

Granddad was the milk brought into the house in steaming buckets and drunk in thick glass goblets. I found it hard to swallow and only managed it with the good things Grandmother cooked to go with it: cherry preserves thick with cherries, fried chicken, biscuits, sausage, gravy, and the yeast bread she sometimes made on Saturday afternoon when everybody else went to the store. She smelled like flour, too, because she powdered her face out of the flour barrel when she went to church or the store.

Anna was the one who did not taste or smell like something to eat. She smelled like the real makeup she put on her face before she went to church or school or out on dates.

Going to School in the Country

Some of my best times on the farm were when I was allowed to go to school with Anna after she began teaching near the farm. Our town schools and the country schools were on a different schedule, so we were often at the farm when Anna was teaching either at Schultztown near Uncle Henry's store, or at Prentiss, the headquarters of Grandmother and Granddad's mail carrier.

School usually lasted from early in the morning to four in the afternoon. The twenty or thirty children ranged in age from four-and five-year-olds to a few grown boys, all in the same room. Along with her Teachers' College training, Anna needed both good judgment and imagination to select the most reliable of the older girls for help with the younger children, nerve enough "when necessary" to use the paddle she kept in her desk drawer (although I never saw her do more than threaten), and all the energy in the world. Physically, she was impressive with the strong arms and broad shoulders of a farm woman who could carry three-gallon buckets of water from the well, or milk half a dozen cows, but she curled her hair, used makeup well, and tried to wear a different pretty wash dress every day because she knew that children "like change." Her first act of the day was to pull the wire that rang the school bell swinging at the top of a pole outside the white or weather-beaten one-room building.

"America" was the patriotic song we sang in those days. And Anna used a pitch pipe as she had been taught in "Public School Music" at Teachers' College to start the children on tune. From the old yellow song book that was used in all the public schools I ever attended in Kentucky and Tennessee, we also sang two or three other songs like "John Brown's Body" and "My Old Kentucky Home," also the Civil War songs, "Yankee Doodle" and "Dixie ." No distinction was made between the two sides in the war when it came to singing. The morning exercises concluded with the children saying "The Lord's Prayer" together.

Anna liked for me to go to school with her because a new face was something else that made a change for the children. I always called her "Aunt Anna" at school though we called her "Anna" at home. She insisted that the girls near my age take turns sitting with me; they all wanted to. Everybody pushed me ahead in the line to get water from the well at noon. She forbade the girl who rode a horse to school from boosting me up on it because she didn't want me to do anything that would scare Mother.

I had books to read from the school library shelf in case I got bored. Anna also thought it was a good example for the children who had not had my "opportunities." I liked the big kids and the little kids all together in the one room, each grade having their own lessons, and then being able to listen to the others. I kept my eyes on *Little Women,* or some other book considered "hard," just long enough to be a good example.

My favorite class was penmanship in which all the children practiced the ovals and push and pulls that Anna modeled on the blackboard. Until she died at the age of 95, I could always recognize her beautiful Palmer Method handwriting on the envelope of a letter.

Anna had frequent singing and games periods both outside and inside school, since neither she nor Mother believed in "making children sit still all the time." The two sisters were more alike than either readily admitted.

I learned as much about how people live in the country from my visits to school with Anna and from my visits with Ila Mae Read, my best friend in the country, as I did about people in the city at the birthday parties that Mary Elizabeth and I went to in Bowling Green.

We called Ila Mae's parents "Miss Cleonis" and "Mr. Orville." They were relatives too distant to be called "aunt" and "uncle" or "cousin," but friends too close to be called "Mr. and Mrs. Read." Ila Mae, just my age, was their only child. I would go home from Sunday School with her one Sunday and be taken home by my family the next. In those weeks, summer after summer, I came to know her as I knew few friends until I was much older.

A little sister that the family had waited several years for, after Ila Mae was born, died when she was four years old. "A perfect little doll," people said. Miss Cleonis had never gotten over the loss. Ila Mae explained to me, "I favor my father, and my little sister favored my mother, and the one you favor is the one who loves you most." But I didn't quite believe it. I believed it even less when Miss Cleonis screamed and fainted as Ila Mae went down to the altar to profess her faith in Christ at one summer's revival meeting. I almost followed her, but hesitated a minute or two because I didn't know whether someone who had been baptized as a baby was supposed to go. I was glad that I was sitting in my seat when Miss Cleonis screamed and I saw her lying on the floor. I would have hated to see my mother lying there. But such a display of emotion proved to me that Ila Mae's mother really did love her.

The first time I spent the night with Ila Mae, we were so excited we stayed awake until midnight talking and giggling, and the next afternoon I had my first experience of "homesickness" which was nearly a real sickness. I did not vomit, but I almost did, and I cried and cried as I lay on a couch looking out the back screen door, thinking of one or another member of the family who might have died while I was having such a good time.

Miss Cleonis and Mr. Orville were both very gentle with me and told me what was wrong: "You're homesick." They urged me to call the farm, which I couldn't bring myself to do. Scared as I was that one of the family had died when I was away, I was even more scared of their fright at hearing me crying over the phone. By the next day when Mr. Orville offered to take me home, I was having such a good time that I didn't want to go.

I loved going to school with Ila Mae, too. As soon as we were out of sight of the house, we took off our shoes and socks and walked down the road, squishing the dust between our toes and stopping now and then to pick a few ripe blackberries. At every lane along the road other children with dinner buckets and bare feet joined us. Ila Mae's parents were the only ones who wouldn't allow their child to leave home without shoes. From all the smiles and laughter, I could see that having a town guest increased her already high prestige.

I was getting old enough to notice that the boys went to much greater lengths to attract my attention than the boys at school back home. Nearly every day when we returned from eating lunch on the school ground, I would hear a ripple of laughter around the room before we quite settled down. Turning around, I saw a boy staring at me with the red-veined underlids of his eyes twisted back over his eyeballs so that he looked blind or dead.

The Reads' house was about half a mile up the bank from Green River. Anna sometimes spent the night there when she came home from college in Bowling Green on a late boat. I have never forgotten that I ate my first catfish at Ila Mae's (my grandfather was not a fisherman; Mr. Orville was). I also have not forgotten the wonderful new clothes smell of the packages from Sears, Roebuck that sometimes came with the mail. It was the smell of the ready-made dresses that Ila Mae's parents could afford for an only child. And it was in the yard off their back porch that I learned to polish the patent leather shoes we wore to Sunday school with one of Miss Cleonis's good fat breakfast biscuits and then feed the crumbs to the Dominecker hens.

After we moved to Tennessee we did not visit at the farm for several years. Ila Mae grew up, moved away from home, and had children of her own. Anna wrote when Miss Cleonis died. I heard later that Mr. Orville had hanged himself in his barn. Miles and miles away, I was still dividing the world of men into the gentle, sweet kind like Mr. Orville who made time for children and the harsher, more businesslike kind who were mostly interested in talking to men.

The Glory that Was Akron, Detroit, Flint

The twenties' prosperity we knew most about was that of friends and relatives who went North to work in the industrial plants.

When a new car pulled up during the night into a neighbor's yard in any of the towns we lived in after Bowling Green, we always knew that somebody's aunt and uncle, or maybe the cousins and grandmother, had just arrived from Akron or Detroit or Flint. It wouldn't be long before one of us would be sent to borrow a cup of sugar or an egg and find out just who they were and how they were getting along. The answer was always "Just fine!" as eyes sparkled.

In the Little Bend, the sons of the local farmers who had gone North to work made much more of a show at church with their families than we did. Every year, among the wagons and buggies with their horses or mules tied to the fence between the church and the woods, were more and more of the newest models of automobiles. I particularly remember the first blue and green models with roll-up windows. "Right off the assembly lines," said the fathers, almost as proud as the sons as they walked around them. The men, women, and children who emerged from the cars all seemed to wear beautiful matching clothes that looked as though they had just come from the store.

These visitors from the North were often among the families that Granddad asked to Sunday dinner. The children took off their white shoes and socks and went barefoot like us. We all took turns with our cousins cranking the ice-cream freezer filled with ice from Beaver Dam. We had lots of time to get acquainted before we gathered around the "second table" after the grown-ups had eaten. We liked hearing as well as they liked telling stories about Santa Claus in the department stores at Christmas and going to the movie palaces on Saturday afternoons. They rode street cars that we had seen only in books. Among all our cousins we were the only ones who had seen actual elephants and giraffes (at a circus with its parade in Bowling Green), but the northern kids could see them any time they liked at the zoos in the big cities. For weeks afterwards we imitated their northern accents.

It was a shock, however, when Anna took some time off from teaching and studying for her degree in Bowling Green to work at one of the rubber companies in Akron. She made up her mind the Sunday that two of her old friends, Arlene and Leroy Fordyce, were in the crowd outside Point Pleasant Church. Leroy was an old student of Mother's and had worked as an extra hand for Granddad until he went to Akron before he was twenty. There was lots of exclaiming and embracing between the two families. I thought Arlene was the prettiest lady I had ever seen, in the most beautiful and impractical clothes. Granddad pumped and pumped on Leroy's hand: "Well, boy—why did it take you so long to get back?" Leroy looked a little choked in his stiff white collar, "To tell you the truth, Mr. Elliott, I didn't want to come until I had something to show for my time." With his pretty wife and his new car, it was plain that he had something to show now.

At dinner Leroy kept urging Anna to come on up to Akron to work. The assembly lines were full of school teachers who were making three or four times as much as they ever did teaching in the country. He turned to his wife, "Honey, did you ever know any sweeter, prettier girls than some of them that worked with you at Goodrich?" Arlene looked more animated than she had since she greeted all of us at church, "I wish you would come, hon. We could have the best old time."

Our mother had never thought much of factories or the people who worked in them. She pictured them primarily, I think, as the sweat shops of New York where women and children burned to death at their sewing machines or as the awful hog and cow butchering establishments of Chicago or Kansas City. She could see that Anna was tempted. As they rushed the food and dishes in and out of the kitchen, she offered her anxious advice, "Now, Anna, don't you let them hurry you into anything. Nobody in our family has ever worked in a factory."

What Mother said would have been true ten years before, but not in the late twenties. She had cousins working at Goodyear. Cousin Willie, Grandmother's niece, whom everybody loved almost as much as they loved Grandmother, had gone to Akron to be near them, and she took in boarders. It would be easy and inexpensive for Anna to go up to live with her and to get one of the readily available jobs when her school was out in February.

We were at the farm when she returned the next July to teach the last of the three years that were necessary for her to get her "life certificate." All of us were out at the end of the lane when the mailman let her out of his car with her suitcases. Mother and Grandmother struggled with one another for the privilege of carrying the second heavy suitcase to the house. We children took turns holding Anna's hand and carrying her pocketbook.

The most exciting part, though, was watching our aunt unpack. Mary Elizabeth and I sat with our eyes wide. We marveled at the new dresses and all the different kinds of underwear with odd names that came out of the suitcases, not just underskirts and bloomers, but teddies, step-ins, lace brassieres, and silk pajamas, nightgowns and satin bedroom slippers with fluffy plumes on them.

She admitted the work on the assembly line was dull, but she enjoyed working with the other women, and she made a better income than she ever did teaching school, or than Mother made with her degree. Living at Aunt Willie's was like being at a co-ed college dormitory with a party going on all the time, and she enjoyed the big department stores in Akron as much as we would have.

As she rearranged the clothes in her closet during the next few days, Mary Elizabeth and I fell heir to many of her older garments which we had always thought were pretty, as well as to bits of makeup left in the dresser drawers from other years. We got all dressed up and made up and went for imaginary rides in the buggy, surrey, or wagon at times when Granddad wasn't likely to be in the barn.

We could hardly wait for people to see Anna in her new clothes her first Sunday back at church. The neighbors and former pupils flocked around her after church, some of them to shake hands, but most to hug her, and one or two to get a little lipstick or mascara on them, which they all laughed about. We heard some of the same things about her teaching that we were used to hearing about Mother's: "I hated school till Miss Anna come along," "The year we had Miss Anna we really learned something." You could see they were glad she was back, but they certainly didn't blame her for having gone away.

In Akron, Anna met Ernest Roberson, the man she was to marry. His visit to the farm was the most engrossing part of the following summer when Anna brought him home. From the beginning he seemed less like a boyfriend and more like somebody you might just know. I can't, for example, remember much about the clothes he wore except that he didn't like to wear a tie, but would put one on for church. He was small like our father, soft-spoken, and put the g's on "i-n-g" words. He had grown up an orphan. Though he fell in love with Anna before he visited the farm, marrying into a family who had lived in the same place since 1896 meant something to him. He did a lot of just walking around with Granddad and his stick and the dog.

Mother couldn't quite forgive Anna's fiancé for being the first factory hand to marry into the immediate family. Still, she granted that he was a success as a tire-builder and made a better living than most men in other lines of work. She insisted that we call him "Uncle Ernest" although we continued to call Anna "Anna."

Just how well off they were during the first years of their marriage we heard about when Anna and Ernest returned to the farm after the Depression hit and stored some of the new furniture they had bought in "Anna's Room." Every month, on the anniversary of their wedding, Ernest had added to what they had started out with by buying something nice. They expected to be able to use the lamps and conveniences for the kitchen like the waffle iron when they got back to a part of the country where they had electricity. Like Mother, Anna loved the advantages of the city. Ernest loved the farm and the solid place in the community a man like Granddad had.

When Ernest was offered his old job again, he and Anna returned to Akron for a short while, but they came back home to run the farm the year that Granddad got very sick, and they remained. As the Miller children grew up, going to visit Grandmother and Granddad also meant going to visit Anna and Ernest and their children at the farm and then in Beaver Dam as their children outgrew the country schools.

The subject of her old friends from the factories, whom Mother seemed to be so prejudiced against, came up sometimes with Anna after Mother died. Many who had left home stuck it out in the North until better times; some who came home for a few years returned to better jobs during the war years. "A lot of them have made real contributions to the community," Anna told me. Several eventually took over their family farms or bought other farms. Leroy and Arlene bought a farm in Florida, and Arlene went back to teaching.

Death, Debt and Dreams

The late twenties were not a time of prosperity for my parents.

Mother loved her children once they were in the world. But she could never have said for any baby after me, "I was so in love, I didn't care." She recognized her sexual drive as strong, and warned her daughters against instincts she feared she had passed on. She and Daddy had agreed to practice abstinence, yet not long after they received their diplomas from Western, Mother found that she was pregnant again.

In the spring of 1927 James William, a second boy, died in the process of being born at the Bowling Green hospital. His head was big and the doctors performed a fetal craniotomy to save Mother's life. Mother was too sick ever to see him, but Daddy pronounced him "perfectly beautiful" and considered entering medical school; he was just thirty and had minored in science at Western, so it was not an entirely outlandish possibility. Mother said that she would stand by him if he really wanted to go. But still owing Cousin Wash the thousand dollars that had brought them to Bowling Green, plus all the hospital bills, they let that dream go.

When Mother was well enough after James William's death, we would sometimes drive around the Bowling Green reservoir on Sunday afternoons and then visit the baby's grave at the cemetery. Mother always cried a little: "You know he died for me." One Sunday she asked Daddy to drive us by the unpretentious brick Cumberland Presbyterian Church which we had never attended: "That's really my church," she said.

She did not mean that we should change churches again, but her illness had given her time for reflection about the life which had been saved. She no longer had to worry about getting pregnant and in her mind she was turning over her procrastination in answering the call to the ministry which she had mentioned to Daddy before they were married.

The outward signs of an inner change are not easy to decipher; still in small ways she began to take more control of her life while she remained mindful of her dreams for us. As soon as she was on her feet, a piano was rented and I took lessons from Professor Strom at Western. We children were almost scared when she came home with her hair cut and a permanent wave like Anna and Miss Evie. Mother had picked her time well; as much as Daddy loved her long hair he couldn't deny her anything that birth-panged year. In the fall after her operation she began taking lessons in oil painting at the college, something she had always wanted to do. She also put in her application at the college employment office for a position teaching Latin.

After having taken time out from his insurance business to be with Mother at the hospital and care for her afterward, Daddy was never able to make the steady income of the friends and relatives who worked in the northern factories. But it wasn't those friends and relatives our smart father had to stand comparison with. The spring that James William was born, Lindbergh made his solo flight across the Atlantic. We celebrated at school and celebrated at home. Lindbergh, six years younger than Daddy, was really "somebody!" Then there was Charlie Chaplin. After Daddy took Mary Elizabeth and me to the college auditorium to see the first talking picture, *The Jazz Singer* with Al Jolson, Mother remembered his taking her to see his favorite actor, Charlie Chaplin. She said that she liked to hear Daddy laugh, but she didn't think Chaplin was a better entertainer than Daddy John would have been, if he had concentrated on that.

Another "somebody" was my father's brother Uncle Era who stopped by Bowling Green on his way home from the Southern Baptist Convention in Louisville after Mother came home from the hospital. Mother remembered having met him in Texas before she and Daddy were married. Her excitement was infectious. He was very well-dressed in a new suit. We loved hearing about our cousins Janice and Spurgeon, named for a famous Baptist minister in England. We also heard about Grandma Susie, still alive and well, and about all the other aunts, uncles, and cousins with names familiar to us. Uncle Era had not done nearly as well in school as Daddy, but here he was, a real power in an important organization like the Southern Baptist Church.

Uncle Henry who ran the country store nearest to my grand-parents' farm was another "somebody" even though he wore over-alls and occasionally used "bad grammar." "More for the common touch," Mother said, "than because he didn't know better."

Even before Mother went to the hospital, there was not enough money to cover the small bills that we ran up at the grocery stores strung out along the highway on the edge of Forest Park. When we ran out of credit at one store we went to another. Mary Elizabeth and I had loved being trusted with an errand to the grocery store back in LeGrande, but now at any time, the owner might grab a shoulder and say, "Tell yo' mammy she owes me $25." When I came back to visit in the neighborhood some years later, one of the owner clerks talked to me in a flatteringly grown-up way until she recognized me. Suddenly her little lashless brown eyes lighted up, "You're John B. Miller's daughter. You tell your Daddy he owes me eleven dollars and twenty-five cents."

I doubt if my parents owed more than two or three thousand dollars. But they owed small amounts to several people who could ill afford to lose anything. And there were the larger bills for school and the hospital. Almost as soon as I learned to read, I was studying the mail which was often left lying around the house. "What does it mean 'Legal action will be taken'," I asked Mother one day when I was about seven. "Well, that means that if we don't pay they will get the law after us." I could almost hear the policeman's step at the door. "But I read a letter like this a long time ago and nothing hap-pened." I had been too scared to ask then. "Well, of course, some-times they just threaten," Mother said.

Mother was as proud of Daddy's lack of "bad habits" as a mother rather than a wife might have been. I remember her repeat-ing again and again for neighbors and friends as well as us: "Your father (or my husband) doesn't smoke or drink or swear. His only bad habit is chewing gum." She added at least once, "That and not paying his bills."

It never seemed fair to me to call them *his* bills; they were the bills of all of us. But a man was supposed to be able to support his family. Daddy himself believed that, as did Grandfather Miller who never owned his own farm and thought of himself as a failure.

Granddad Elliott believed it, though he tried not to come out and say it. Mother seemed to believe it when she spoke of "his" bills.

Daddy was exhilarated when he made a sale and continued to feel that his best chance of making a living was out on the road selling. Even though she resented the expense of the car, Mother continued to hope that selling was the talent with which he could support the family.

If the mail brought nightmares during our last years in Bowling Green, it also brought beautiful daydreams. The insurance company addressed a brochure to its salesmen: "Who Lives in the House at the Top of the Hill?" It carried a dirigible of dreams. The picture of an elegant well-matched living room was the setting for one corner of the life indoors that Mary Elizabeth and I hoped for. The shine of the kitchen and bathroom lighted up the whole place, and though piano playing was permitted, you could still hear the ring of a telephone. The well-dressed father, so happy in the knowledge of being a good provider, would never yell at the mother or the children; he would like what the mother cooked and entertain friends like men in the funny papers. We hoped for some kind of change in Mother, too. Of course, she might be a Sunday School teacher: I thought of the beautifully dressed women in the big churches in Bowling Green. She could read Latin in her room if she liked, provided she didn't talk about it with people who thought she was putting on. I began a continued daydream about this family which moved whenever we did.

A priority for Mother as she began thinking about her first teaching position after she received her degree was to move to a place where Daddy could easily come home on weekends. In late 1927 he thought it would be the eastern part of the state and Mother was unexpectedly offered a position teaching Latin in Harlan, Kentucky beginning in January 1928.

A Funeral at Christmas

We had not planned to spend Christmas of 1927 at my grandfather's farm.

Santa Claus was to bring Mary Elizabeth and me the dolls with hair and eyes and the doll buggies that Mother had been determined her little girls would have ever since she was a child. There was no way gifts as large as the buggies could be transported with four children over the forty miles of winter-treacherous roads from Bowling Green to the Little Bend.

The first days of vacation from Mary Elizabeth's first grade and my third in school were bright and cold. With the long convalescence after James William's death and the operation that followed, Mother was enjoying her first break from teaching, going to school, and having babies since I was born. She wanted to make it a perfect Christmas. She had finally indulged in our first set of electric tree lights and turned them on in the cold front room of the Bowling Green house each time Mary Elizabeth and I made our brief goose-bumpy forays to add more paper chains and strings of popcorn to the ceiling-high Christmas tree.

Then on the evening of December 22, a neighbor knocked on the door to call Mother to her phone. Uncle Henry Elliott who ran the store at Schultztown had died after a year's illness. We would have Christmas at the farm after all.

Fortunately, Daddy had come home early that day, and he and Mother had us packed and in the car while it was still dark the next morning. At the last minute I saw Mother put behind the back seat the packages that I would recognize later as the doll boxes. Mary Elizabeth and I barely had time to wonder how Santa Claus would know that we had left home, but we had faith that he was as all-seeing as God.

It was a nice day and we would have arrived at the farm by evening, except for the last ten miles of ruts and mud. Mother began apologizing soon after we left Beaver Dam and complimenting Daddy's good driving as he wrestled with the steering wheel. Finally he stopped spinning his wheels in one of the deepest mud holes and went to find a farmer who could bring his lantern and his mules to drag us out.

We were exhausted when we pulled up in front of Grand-dad's barn, but still felt the big thump of happiness that was always there when we finally got to the farm. The fires were lit in all the fireplaces of the house, and Anna had gone out that afternoon and cut a Christmas tree and had it in place and decorated.

Aunt Allye, Uncle Robert and our cousin Lucille were already there. Uncle Henry's family consisting of Aunt Barbara, J.G., and Dorcas would be along Christmas Eve for the funeral.

The crowd had waited supper for us, and nobody cried except for a few tears when the sisters and Grandmother kissed and when Grandmother brought out Mother's favorite cherry preserves to go with the hot biscuits.

It was surprising that there was always enough room for any number of people to sleep in my grandparents' house. Aunt Allye's family slept in Anna's room. Our family slept in the Girls' Room where the five Elliott sisters, who were now only three, slept when they were children. As Mary Elizabeth, Caroline and I dropped off to sleep in one of the high head-boarded double beds, I kept trying to think of Uncle Henry, but visions of dolls, sugar plums, and my relatives still alive kept dancing in my head.

Not that I didn't love Uncle Henry. When Mother told the story of his death to new acquaintances over and over in later years, as she told those of her sisters, Evie and Edna, she talked about his "big way"—"never met a stranger in his life." He killed himself being so accommodating, always carrying those big sacks of feed and chicken coops for his customers in Schultztown.

If Mother envied Anna for the nice things Granddad could afford for her in the more prosperous times of Anna's childhood, Anna envied Mother for having had a big brother at home at least for a part of her youth. Mother and Aunt Edna had someone besides Granddad to take them to the play parties in the neighborhood or anywhere else they wanted to go. She could remember his and Aunt Barbara's wedding and how as a little girl she had run back and forth between the front room and the kitchen to report everything happening to Aunt Evie who was confined to her chair or her cradle.

Uncle Henry was a big man who weighed more than 200 pounds, and every Saturday afternoon in the summer when we took the three-mile ride in the wagon to the store, we could hear his laugh a quarter of a mile away. The store was as much a community institution as any of the churches and schools, maybe more, because the community had several churches and schools between the Green River and Prentiss where the mail came in, but only one store.

Mary Elizabeth and I liked nothing better than spending the night with our cousin Dorcas before Uncle Henry got sick and the family moved to Beaver Dam. I can remember thinking that being a country storekeeper with access to the candy counter, and all those friends coming and going, would be the most exciting job in the world.

His funeral packed Point Pleasant Church which Granddad had helped to build. Fortunately there had been a freeze overnight, so the roads were passable.

Still we had a long wait for the undertakers to roll the coffin in and put the flowers in place, more flowers than anyone had ever seen in that church. We kept hearing one car and then another stop outside and more people arriving. The whole family remained proud for the rest of their lives of the wonderful show of flowers. When they opened the casket we had the last chance to look at our uncle and the first chance of our lives to look at someone dead.

Mother even held little brother John up to look. She believed in children knowing about death, and as we grew up took us to every funeral she could persuade us to go to. I was a little ashamed that I couldn't cry like Mary Elizabeth, but I was too much in awe of the stillness of the man I remembered as so noisily alive. My cousins were now "orphans," a word I knew from the Bible and fairy stories. Aunt Barbara was "a widow."

Great wet snow flakes were falling in the twilight when Uncle Henry's casket was lowered into the grave beside the sisters who had died so many years before. When the blanket, wreaths, and sprays of flowers were all heaped on the grave, somebody took a snapshot and gave it to Mother. Somehow she found time to make an oil painting of the grave with all the flowers and gave it to Grandmother for a present the following Christmas. It replaced her diploma above the mantel in Anna's Room.

Back at Grandmother and Granddad's, everybody felt sorry for the cousins as well as for Uncle Henry's children for having to go through the funeral at Christmas time. Daddy was more comfortable with the men in the family than I had ever seen him before. They worked hard at entertaining us. After supper Uncle Robert, Granddad and Daddy took us out on the side porch of the house and shot Roman candles into the snow. They also lit sparklers for any of us that weren't too scared to hold them.

Then Johnny Hawes, the hired man who slept on a cot in the kitchen, gathered all of us around the kitchen fireplace and helped us crack hickory nuts and walnuts on the hearth. He sang some of the old songs he knew.

Dorcas who was six years old, like Mary Elizabeth, seemed really to enjoy it all, too. But J.G., who had his fifteenth birthday that very day, stood in the background looking sad and finally went into the living room to remember his father with the grown-ups.

Aunt Barbara and J.G. smiled as they opened their presents Christmas morning. I somehow remember that J.G. got a gun and that Uncle Robert was going to take him hunting. Aunt Barbara smiled even more as Grandmother hugged her for the beautiful dresser scarf she had embroidered for her. Getting our dolls was the wonderful part of the day for Mary Elizabeth and me. We liked Grandmother's biscuits and sausage for breakfast even better than the candy everybody had expected us to eat too much of.

Back home in Bowling Green, Mother took our doll buggies out of the closet where she had hidden them. Pleased as she was, Mary Elizabeth couldn't help asking, "Is Santa Claus real?"

"Santa Claus is a spirit," Mother said, "and spirits are real."

Chapter II

After Bowling Green

Harlan, where Mother took her first position teaching after her long illness, was in the coal producing mountains of eastern Kentucky. We lived on the second floor of what we thought of as "a real apartment building," across the street from the county courthouse. We were proud of the hot and cold running water in the kitchen and bathroom, the electric kitchen stove, and the only telephone we would ever have at home. On Saturday picnics we learned words like "mountain laurel," "rhododendron" and "paw-paw."

Mother loved teaching Latin full-time at Harlan High School in a position passed on to her by a teacher killed in an accident during Christmas vacation. She could have continued in the fall, but Daddy was not getting home as often as they had both hoped when we moved, and always haunted by the death of her little sister Evie, Mother believed the mountain air might be to blame for the asthma I developed. She also hated the size of our milk and grocery bills in a town where we could not have a cow and a garden. When Daddy's business in the fall seemed to be centered near Louisville, she took a job in Chaplin not far from Bardstown and the Old Kentucky Home. We went back to an outside toilet and water from a well. And there was room for a garden and a place to tether a cow in the yard. Our piano teacher asked us to dinner in her big brick house, said to have been built with money from the sale of a family race horse. Afterwards, in my mind the "Little Colonel" and other southern heroines up to Scarlett O'Hara lived in this house.

I continued to have asthma and had to stay home the day teachers and students heard Herbert Hoover inaugurated to the presidency on a radio brought to school. Mother came home thrilled and told us that the modern age we were coming into was going to be a wonderful time.

As the country moved into 1929, Daddy's insurance manager was having troubles. In discussions that continued over several of his trips home to Chaplin, he and Mother finally agreed about the uncertainty of a salesman's income and the inevitability of his expenses. The decision was made that Mother would resign her position in Chaplin, and she and Daddy would again take jobs teaching together. This time they would work in Hiseville, where Daddy would be principal of a four-year high school with several teachers under him and Mother would teach Latin and English.

Hiseville was another little town off the paved road, actually not far from LeGrande, but larger. With their two salaries Mother and Daddy hoped not only to cover our regular expenses but to start paying their debts. We had a cow, a pig, a garden, and our first piano. Our piano teacher, Mrs. Forrest, was interested in many of the same religious questions as Mother and became one of the best women friends of her life. Daddy kept his car and directed a play, *Eyes of Love,* early in the fall. And he had not forgotten his farm skills. One Saturday morning he tied and hung up our hog and cut its throat. In the next weeks we ate more meat than we had ever eaten in our lives.

Up and down the one main street of town we knew everybody's name. The elderly brother and sister who lived across the street regularly brought us cookies and gave a standing invitation to the whole family to listen to *Amos and Andy* on the radio every week.

Best of all for me was my first "best friend," an only child named Corinne who lived a few doors away. We played at our house even more than at hers, since Mother liked us to include Caroline and John B. in our dress-up games. They were based on books which Mother had arranged to have mailed from the Louisville Free Public Library and that Corinne read as eagerly as I did.

As comfortable as we were, the decision of both parents to change vocations took us away from Hiseville.

New Vocations:
The Ministry and the Oil Business

Along with those stories about high wages in the North, stories we liked to hear wherever grown-ups gathered, were those about oil in Oklahoma. We liked thinking about people getting rich overnight as much as the adults did, although the Oklahoma oil wells seemed very far away.

Soon after we arrived in Hiseville, we were hearing about a little oil and gas boom in our part of the state. A number of people were making money and they weren't Indians either, but people like the grandparents and parents of the school children in places we had lived.

Once he got his degree, I think Mother could have been content for Daddy to spend the rest of his life as a small-town school principal. Had the Hiseville job offered the money and the status that were necessary for his self respect—certainly it offered other interests—Daddy might have been content to go on living in that remote little town. Teachers of all ranks throughout the nation were poorly paid, however, in comparison with successful business and professional men. There was still that debt to Cousin Wash, and from month to month my parents' salaries never stretched as far as they hoped. Daddy found more to be displeased about with us children than he ever had before. I could not move fast enough one evening when he asked me to move a chair to the supper table and received spanks on the bottom which I had not experienced since I was a small child. The spanks could not have hurt much, but I thought I was too old to be whipped and did not forgive him for a long time.

After a few months things gradually began to change. Daddy had begun to be away a good many weekends as he drove out into the area where the oil activity was going on, especially near our old community of LeGrande. His temper and the bad stomach which had been troubling him improved as he reacquainted himself with old friends and neighbors. He was also getting to know people who had land to lease as well as some oil men from Louisville who were leasing and bringing in oil rigs.

Mother had less to say about the debts and the car as Daddy became more absorbed in his new interest, but we could tell something was changing for her, too. She had long periods of preoccupation when she did not speak or sing, and she did much of the family cooking with a Bible in her hand.

Although Daddy did not accompany us, Mother and we children had settled down to Sunday School and church at his family church, the Christian. Mother particularly liked the opportunity for her children to take Communion every Sunday. The congregation got used to the long pause required for four children and Mother to take and return the little glasses to the tray when Communion was served. One Sunday we skipped church in town and Daddy drove us to a Cumberland Presbyterian church Mother had heard about several miles out in the country. After we arrived at the isolated little country church, the kind we thought Mother didn't like except in the Little Bend, Daddy and Caroline and John B. stayed in the car with the Sunday papers; Mary Elizabeth and I accompanied Mother into the church. After the sermon we met the preacher and some of the more devout members of the congregation. When they heard Mother was a Cumberland Presbyterian they called her "Sister" and spoke in what sounded like bits and pieces of sermons in country voices such as we knew Mother hoped we would not grow up with.

One of the members was a gaunt unsmiling man who walked with a cane. Mother took him to the car to meet Daddy who recognized him as someone he had sold insurance to in the past. They shook hands. Mother asked the man, his wife, and one or two other church members to come to our noontime meal, dinner, the following Saturday.

Daddy was away in the oil fields the day the carload of country church members arrived for their first dinner. We children rushed out to the car to greet them. Daddy's old acquaintance was the driver. The group was barely out of the car and making their way to the front door when he pointed his cane at me, "Is that girl saved?"

Mother answered quickly, "Why yes, she was baptized when she was a baby."

"I mean, has she had the conviction of sin and given her heart to the Lord?"

Mother managed to distract him by asking him to come in for a cup of coffee. She didn't mean for anyone to scare us or push us too hard about religion. But the question he asked was one that had disturbed me. Had we been saved by being baptized as babies? As friends like Ila Mae went down the aisle when the invitation to the altar was given at one or another of the many revival meetings we children attended with our parents, I kept hoping that salvation was another something special that Mother and Daddy had been able to give us. Although he never spoke about it again, the man with the cane exacerbated the anxiety I continued to feel for years.

Mother and her friends formed a regular Saturday prayer group. After lunch in the kitchen they dragged their chairs into the living room and knelt with their faces in their hands. We children tried to keep out of the way, but sometimes I found myself reading a book in the bedroom. Through the half-open door, I could see into the living room and more than once I saw the man whom I continued to dislike pounding his fist on the seat of the chair at which he was kneeling: "Sister Miller, if you have had the 'Call,' there's just no way you can run away from it."

Finally one day in our after-school talk I asked Mother what the "Call" was. Mother explained that God had a way of speaking to people whom He had chosen to be ministers. He had chosen her for the "Call." "I am going to do something a lot more wonderful than teach. I am going to be a minister."

My words popped out: "But women can't be ministers." I had never seen a woman minister and, for the moment, could not remember having even heard of one.

"Whatever gave you that idea?" She was almost angry that a daughter of hers, however young, had such a low estimate of women. "Women can do anything men can do and they shouldn't let men tell them they can't."

The next time Mary Elizabeth and I were sent on an errand alone together, I told her what Mother had told me. Her first reaction was the same as mine: "Can women be ministers?"

How we both wished they couldn't, that there were some law that would hold Mother down and force her to be more like other mothers. Mary Elizabeth said, "Let's don't tell anyone," and I agreed.

I brought up the subject after school with Mother again. "I'll bet you and Daddy could get a job teaching in Louisville or Lexington or one of those northern towns like Flint or Akron." I was ashamed to tell her that we were ashamed to have a mother who was a minister. Mother was sympathetic and put her arms around me: "Darling, I have no choice. I am doing what God wants me to do." I pulled away from her and began to cry, "Oh, I wish that you had never met that awful man. I know that he is persuading you to do something you would never have thought of if he hadn't come along."

Mother remained calm: "No, darling, I have been telling myself that I would be a minister ever since I was a little girl and your father gave his consent before we were married. I have been looking around for someone to help me have the courage to do what I want to do." She told me that the man with the cane had regretted for years that he had not left his father's farm to preach, and he was trying to keep her from making the same mistake. She also told me that she was planning to attend the next meeting of the Logan Presbytery, the group of pastors and lay people who governed the church in our area, and looking forward to being accepted as a candidate for the ministry. It would be in Bowling Green and she would like me to go with her.

I think Mary Elizabeth and I felt that our mother's new profession had been "sprung" on us partly because she had always shared so much with us. This most important secret she had kept hidden for the first decade of our lives. I was now ten and Mary Elizabeth nine. We never learned exactly when the call to preach came. We did know about her experience of conversion which occurred when she was sixteen. She had always wanted it, as most people did for both themselves and their children, "because I had seen people whom God had changed so that they were entirely different, all made over with complete confidence and trust. I didn't have that." She never forgot the surge of happiness and illumination she felt after she made her profession of faith at a revival meeting at what my Aunt Anna told me was the Baptist church, the other church in the Little Bend. She was baptized at Point Pleasant, the Cumberland Presbyterian family church.

Surely Mary Elizabeth and I never quite listened when Mother told us about Mrs. Louisa Woosley, "the first Cumberland Presbyterian woman minister." Grandmother and Granddad, as well as Mother, remembered vividly the woman they called "Sister Woosley" who preached for years without official permission of the church. She was already well known as a powerful evangelist when she held a revival meeting at Point Pleasant Church some time after Mother was old enough to pay attention. It would be many years before she read *Shall Women Preach? Or the Question Answered,* the book Mrs. Woosley published in 1891. But everybody knew Mrs. Woosley's story: how she became convinced that "God, being no respecter of persons, has a great work for women to do. I felt 'Woe is me if I preach not the gospel'." The photograph in her book, taken in her early preaching days, shows her as a beautiful young woman. Her authority and her quiet voice stayed with Mother: "She talked in a conversational tone and people believed, so quiet and gentle she was."

If that first contact with a woman minister was crucial in Mother's call to the ministry, so was the first serious discussion of women's suffrage which she heard at the University of Kentucky. Women who were "somebody" spoke about it in public. One of them was Frances McVey, Vassar '13, wife of the president of the University of Kentucky. Mother believed in the principles of the movement immediately, "because they were right"; the suffragettes said what she had always believed.

Mother's love of study and especially Latin had some bearing on her "Call." The Constitution of the Cumberland Presbyterian Church, first formulated in 1815, stated that "It is highly reproachful to religion and dangerous to the church to entrust the ministry to weak and ignorant men." It recommended that ministers should "know Latin, at least, and New Testament Greek and Hebrew if possible." After she was given the gold medal for excelling in Latin at Hartford College, she majored in it at Teachers' College, and it was the subject she taught with most pleasure during many later years as a teacher.

Instead of returning to the University of Kentucky after a term there, she followed the suggestion of a professor who told her that she should do something about the hesitation in her speech. She was very conscious of the defect. Could someone who expected to be a minister stammer? She still blamed herself for having imitated another child's stammer when she was in country school, and now spent a summer term, maybe two terms, at the Bogue Institute for Stammerers in Indianapolis. The dumbbells with which she practiced the speech therapy exercises she had learned there were among the first things placed on the moving van each time we moved.

Inviting me to go with her to that Presbytery meeting in Bowling Green was an inspired gesture toward winning my acquiescence, if not my enthusiasm, for what I saw as a hateful decision. We all loved Bowling Green and going anywhere alone with Mother was a very special privilege. The meeting took place in the church building which we had decided against when we moved to Bowling Green. Even though it was not as grand as the big Christian and Presbyterian churches, it was built of brick and was much more substantial than the small Cumberland Presbyterian churches we had seen in the country. Lunch both days of the meeting was served in the Sunday School building. I liked the pretty salads and the sandwiches with the crusts neatly removed that the women of the church served. Mother and I were lodged for the night in an elegant home with embroidered curtains at the windows, and our soft voiced, marcelled hostess was one of those women Mary Elizabeth and I wished Mother could be like.

The preachers who had come together for the meeting mostly talked in the country way of our visitors from near Hiseville. Mother explained, as we were getting ready to go to bed at the elegant house, a major reason for the Cumberland Presbyterian split-off from the mother church in the early 1800s. It was the impracticability of the Presbyterian insistence that young men who received the "Call" should return East, preferably to Princeton, for their theological educations. Those rural accents went back a long way.

Both the rural and town-talking preachers and church members were respectful of Mother. They called her "Sister Miller" and invited her to pray in the public meetings at least two or three times during the two days we were there. I played "In the Garden" on the piano at one of the services and received compliments and pats on the head, "God bless you, honey." The necessary number agreed to back Mother for membership in the Presbytery if she still felt the "Call" a year from then.

On the way home I asked why we had attended the other churches in Bowling Green when we lived there instead of the Cumberland Presbyterian. Mother explained, "I wanted you to have the experience of that kind of church then. Remember the beautiful Sunday School papers you brought home? Now I think I will stand a better chance in my own church."

Mrs. Woosley was not the only woman Cumberland Presbyterian minister who preached without official permission of the church, but she was the best known and the first allowed ordination. By 1920 when the national suffrage amendment was passed, five more women had been ordained. Then in 1921, "to bring our Constitution into harmony with our present practice," the General Assembly of the Cumberland Presbyterian Church passed the resolution initiated by an elder from Mrs. Woosley's Owensboro Presbytery:

The word 'man' with respect to a human being is a generic term and as used in the Holy Scriptures and Constitution and confessional statements of the Church has no reference to sex, and should be construed to, and does in fact, include the human being whether male or female.

Not until 1955, thirty-four years after the Cumberland Presbyterian, did the Presbyterian Church, U.S.A., the denomination of the handsome Bowling Green church, pass a similar resolution admitting women to the ministry.

During the summer we began to take it for granted that Mother would indeed someday become a minister. After we heard about the wedding plans of our Aunt Anna, and soon-to-be Uncle Ernest, when we went to the farm in the summer, "Wedding" became a favorite dress-up game. Some of Daddy's old clothes were added to the dress-up box for the men's costumes and Mother made available to us the actual words for the "Solemnization of Marriage" from the Cumberland Presbyterian Confession of Faith. Caroline and John B. were allowed to carry the mosquito netting that was the bridal veil;

Mary Elizabeth, Corinne, and I took turns being bride, groom, and preacher.

While continuing as principal the second year in Hiseville, Daddy became more thoroughly entrenched in the oil business, and he seemed to have additional energy for his school work. He even put on a minstrel show in which he was an end man, wore a flat straw hat and told jokes. Mother sang in the chorus; Mary Elizabeth and I learned to do the Charleston. We all wore black faces and kept sheets and towels smutted up at home for some time, especially since requests for the show came from both LeGrande and Horse Cave.

Daddy liked the people he had to deal with in the oil business, and he especially liked the fact that real money was involved. Early in the spring of 1931, he brought home one of the new Ford Model A cars. He had finally made the connection with a Mr. Wilson of Louisville that looked like the chance he had been waiting for. The car was a kind of promise that we were going to realize our dream of being "like other people." When Mr. Wilson offered him a full-time job, Mother said that she would stay at home and keep house if Daddy would make the living, a promise none of us ever expected to hear from her. Having taught for two years, they both handed in their resignations to the Hiseville High School in the spring of 1931, one of the worst years of the Depression.

Another Move

We planned to move to Horse Cave, a more substantial town than Hiseville and nearer the oil fields, as soon as school was out. Daddy and Mother put money down on a house in Horse Cave that would have been the nicest we had ever lived in. The four of us children had a chance to see it when we took the minstrel show to Horse Cave. The afternoon of the dress rehearsal Daddy got the key from the agent to show it to us. On the way to the agent's office, we saw that it was on the best street in town and set in a yard with good grass. The house was brick with a pretty white scroll trim around the porch. When Daddy unlocked the front door, we tiptoed into the empty front room as though it were a church. We noticed first the chandelier in the middle of the living room ceiling. Then we moved into the kitchen where there was a sink with faucets for hot and cold water. Somebody had already found the bathroom. The radiators indicated the house was heated by a furnace.

Everything was going to be beautiful, even better than having all the meat we could eat, all the books we could read, and Corinne for a best friend. We would have our debts paid and the house on the top of the hill. As we rejoiced in these things that seemed like a dream, including the new car, I said to Mother one day, "Isn't it strange that when everybody else is talking about a Depression and losing their jobs, we are better off than we've ever been?" Mother agreed that the difference between us and other people was strange, but pointed out: "Your father has been keeping his eyes open and it is about time for some good fortune to come his way."

Then mysteriously, the night before our parents were to sign the papers for it, the house with the chandelier burned down. Mother was hesitant about telling us, almost as if somebody we cared about had died, but she refused to take it hard herself: "I don't know how it is, but some way the Lord's hand is in it." She and Daddy decided that maybe they had better not put that money into a down payment on another house. Looking for a house to rent, we went by the burned place; only ashes were left, and a big chimney, like scenes from the Civil War. The little house that we later moved to was on the edge of Horse Cave and was more like the houses we had always lived in.

The school year was longer in Horse Cave than in Hiseville. Mary Elizabeth and I had already passed into the next grade when we moved, and now we had to go back to our same grade for several weeks. Caroline went into first grade and did so well that she was able to enter second grade when we moved to McKenzie. I had to master a whole book of Kentucky history which was a required subject for sixth grade in Horse Cave.

Mother seemed more relaxed as a housewife and minister-to-be than she had been as a teacher. She would even sit down and have coffee with the woman who lived next door. There was a big cherry tree in the yard, and she canned cherries as lavishly as she worked with blackberries at the farm. I missed Corinne, but it never occurred to me to protest or to wish things were different. Moving, like illness or accidents, simply happened to you.

Among the choices of Protestant churches in Horse Cave we went to the Methodist, Grandmother's family church before she was married. I remember listening seriously to the sermons of the preacher. I realized I was becoming more interested in religious matters in general. My Sunday School teacher came to visit and brought a copy of H.G. Wells's *Outline of History* for me to read. Mother was proud that such a well-educated woman had the idea that an eleven-year-old would want to read such an obviously adult book. She was not disturbed about my learning about "dinosaurs" as she had been when she was shown the *pythecanthropus erectus* at the University of Kentucky. She told me that it had never occurred to her that "educated people believed in evolution." She did not know much about it then, but when I asked how dinosaurs fit into the story of creation in Genesis, she said, "The Bible does not tell us how long God's days are."

Another improvement in Horse Cave over the towns we had lived in was its moving picture theater. Mary Elizabeth and I went as often as Mother allowed us to go to the films that were based on a book. We missed a number of Corinne's and my favorite movie stars like Clara Bow, Joan Crawford, and Jean Harlow, but saw *Huckle-*

berry Finn, Cimarron, and *Daddy Long Legs.*

All four of us children went to Presbytery on the momentous occasion when Mother was licensed as a candidate for the ministry. So as not to take Daddy away from his business, Mother managed a ride to the one-room white clapboarded church where the Presbytery was held. Daddy appeared in the new car when it was time to leave so that we could take Mrs. Forrest, our Music and Expression teacher from Hiseville, to visit Grandmother and Granddad after Presbytery. Mrs. Forrest had used her talents extensively in gospel work and was in charge of the music for the occasion. She had supported Mother in her decision to be a minister, and Mother counted on her to help Granddad and Grandmother see how serious her Call was.

As in her graduation from college, Mother's having four children when she joined the Presbytery was praised with reserved wonder. Unlike some career women who chose to keep their children in the background, Mother could not hide her pride in us and was eager to have us meet the new people whom she believed would be important in her life. We preferred to concentrate on the deviled eggs and chocolate cake at the Dinner-on-the-Ground to being passed around as the children of Sister Miller, the woman who had joined the Presbytery. We were glad when Daddy appeared in the new car to make it clear that we also belonged to a world of men and cars.

We did have to stay over one night and we were too many to be housed with one family. Mary Elizabeth and I stayed together with a family who lived in a log cabin. We had never slept in an actual log cabin before and it raised Mother's new vocation a little in our eyes, just as sleeping in a southern mansion would have. During the night I woke up needing to go to the toilet and lay in bed beside Mary Elizabeth for a long time trying to convince myself that I could wait until morning. Finally I knew I couldn't and stepped with bare feet on the moonlit floor, pushed open the screen door, and squatted on the earth beside the strange house. I smelled the warm pee, felt the cold slickness of the dirt, and looked at the huge moon in the sky. My mother was going to be a preacher. I could hardly believe it.

Mother need not have worried about Grandmother and Granddad's acceptance of her "Call." At Point Pleasant they had a big Dinner-on-the-Ground to celebrate Mother's joining the Presbytery and the presence of our Hiseville music teacher in the community. Mrs. Forrest played the organ. The sermon that Mother had preached at Presbytery she gave to old friends and neighbors. They all took it for granted that of course Mr. Elliott's daughter, "Miss Mary," could preach if she wanted to. Sister Woosley, a kind of guardian angel, was still remembered in the community where she had preached more than twenty years before.

Before Mother's sermon, and at Mrs. Forrest's urging, I gave "Tommy's Prayer," her favorite among the readings on which she had coached me. It was a poem in thirty quatrains about a crippled boy whose prayer to die and leave his drunken mother is granted. Toward the end of the piece, I was startled to hear, along with all the more general nose-blowings in the audience, a loud sob. It was from Granddad, sitting near the back as he usually did, and rubbing his eye with his big thumb. Much as I liked a responsive audience, I felt a little ashamed that a child like me could get up before grown-ups and make them cry. I certainly had not expected it from Granddad. I think it made me a little more shy of him, but it also made him a little more aware of me. When I got asthma after a happy afternoon of sliding on a new haystack and was put to bed on the davenport in Anna's Room he came in to visit me at the end of the day as he had once visited Aunt Evie.

John Brison Miller in the cavalry uniform he was wearing when he walked into Mary Elliott's school room in January 1919

Uncle Bob Miller and John Brison Miller, 1920

Mary Elliott Miller and first daughter, U.T., 1920

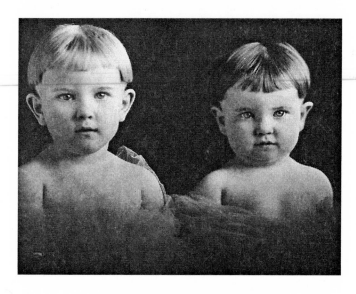

U.T. and Mary Elizabeth, 1923

The three girls with dolls,
U.T. and Mary Elizabeth standing, Caroline sitting
Bowling Green, 1926

Graduation, Western Kentucky State Teachers College, 1926
Back row: Mary Miller, Mary Elizabeth, John Miller and Caroline
Front row: U.T. and John Brison

U.T., 1936, photograph
included in application for
admission to Vassar

Boyce Alexander Gooch,
Memphis, early '40s

Cecil M. Gooch,
early '40s

U.T.

Mary Elizabeth

Caroline

John Brison, Jr.

The four Miller children in the early 1940s

Mary Elliott Miller, graduation with theological degree
Bethel College, 1960

Point Pleasant Cumberland Presbyterian Church in the Little Bend which Grandfather Elliott helped to build. Here Mary Elliott Miller was baptized, heard Mrs. Louisa M. Woosley preach, and delivered her own first sermon.

Chapter III

Cotton Country

Before we all went to Presbytery, Mother and Daddy knew that he was no longer in the oil business. Mr. Wilson, the oil executive with whom he had been on such good terms, died about the time we moved to Horse Cave, and Daddy did not have the same relationship with Mr. Wilson's sons. At the same time, the Kentucky oil boom was essentially over; the first wells in the area were giving out, few new ones were coming in, and the price of oil was going down. Our father informed Mother that he had to find another way of making a living.

In one of our many family discussions later about "what happened," my brother John argued vehemently that at this point Daddy should have "put his foot down and taken charge." Our parents should have looked for other teaching jobs. But school boards were no longer hiring married women anywhere in the nation, and Mother could not have gotten another job. Daddy might have gotten one eventually. But neither he nor Mother looked.

Of course neither knew how really bad the times were, but I am convinced that Daddy was somewhat relieved, and maybe even proud, that rather than Mother's being devastated by his loss of what had looked like the job of his dreams, she had a dream of her own. At the same time that Logan Presbytery elected her as a licentiate for the ministry, Mother was named as their candidate for study at the Cumberland Presbyterian Church's seminary at Bethel College in McKenzie, Tennessee. Daddy must have agreed to her going to school in McKenzie before we all went to Presbytery. He saw going on the road and selling as a possible profession and Tennessee as good a place as Kentucky for him to come and go from home.

On one of his last trips to the oil fields that summer of 1931, Daddy brought us a little brown dog that we named "Brownie." Mary Elizabeth stayed on after Presbytery at Grandmother and Granddad's and raised the chickens that started the bank account with which she hoped to buy a bicycle. None of the rest of us shed a tear when we left Horse Cave. Mother and Daddy made the move as easy and inexpensive as possible by storing furniture, toys, and books in an attic room of the house we had been living in. Into that nice car bought in the spring, they packed the essential clothes, bed clothes, family photographs, our cat and four kittens, and the brown puppy. Mother also got at least two dozen quarts of her cherries into the trunk of the car in which Daddy drove us to McKenzie.

We drove through Bowling Green and Nashville, then west across the loop of the Tennessee River that separates West Tennessee from Middle Tennessee. In front of the state capitol of Tennessee in Nashville Daddy promised that some day each of us might see the capitols of all the states of the union. Beyond Nashville he insisted on stopping for the first barbecue sandwiches we had ever eaten, in spite of Mother's protest that she had brought biscuits and jam for lunch. The tall man at the Tennessee River toll bridge was shocked in a friendly way at all the children and animals in the car and threatened to charge toll on the kittens.

The biggest thrill was seeing our first cotton: "What is that white stuff in the fields?"

"Why, you know what that is. That's cotton."

"We didn't know we were going to see cotton."

Daddy stopped the car, stepped over a barbed wire fence, and picked bolls for Caroline, John B., and me. The whiteness and softness of the bolls matched the clouds in the blue sky; they were as exotic as coconuts. He had often told us stories about the grand trips his father and big brothers took south from the Texas Panhandle to pick cotton, following the crop north. He spent years waiting to be grown up enough to take off with them in the family wagon which was also a camp wagon. The cotton rush was as fine an adventure as any gold rush.

As the car moved further into West Tennessee, the towns among the fields got a little closer together. We passed one town after another that I knew Mary Elizabeth would be glad was not our town, passed any number of houses I thought she would like. Finally, down some dips and up some rises, we saw the "Welcome to McKenzie" sign. As we drove past the garages and the backs of the hotels and other businesses, the paved highway blended smoothly with the paved streets. There was no courthouse. "This is a college town, not a county seat," said Mother.

The town spread out in a network of shaded streets with brick and frame houses, most of them with gabled roofs, porches across the front, and some flowers on the borders of neatly mowed lawns. With all the towns we had lived in, one of the things I had always missed was a "hometown," and I immediately decided that McKenzie was it. It wasn't too big nor too small, neither outstandingly rich nor poor. It wasn't beautiful nor quaint, but it wasn't ugly either, and the trees and sidewalks gave it a dignified pattern. The cotton had prepared me to look for signs of the old South. At the intersection of Stonewall and Magnolia streets was a yellow brick two-story mansion with white pillars.

"We are going to like this town," I announced to Mother and Daddy from the backseat beside Caroline and John B. As we drove through the town square and the main streets of town, we did not see the back streets where the Negro people lived with their own churches and school. We also missed Brawnertown on the road to Memphis where the white sharecroppers and tenants, pushed off the soil-depleted farms by the low price of cotton, were huddled in shanties.

Daddy and Mother took what pleasure they could on a hot August afternoon in their eldest child's approval of the town, and against my father's desire to drive around until he found Bethel, Mother opened the car door and inquired the way from a passer-by. Nothing was very far from anything else in McKenzie, and soon we were on the gravel driveway in front of the main building where Mother was to begin work on her ministerial degree.

I imagined Mary Elizabeth saying, "Is that Bethel?" Our notion of what a college ought to look like was the acropolis on the top of the highest hill in Bowling Green that was Western Kentucky State Teachers' College. In the early thirties Bethel looked more like a high school with a couple of extra buildings. Mother, who had seen pictures of the college in church magazines, was unsurprised: "We aren't a rich school."

Mother and Daddy introduced themselves at the college office and were given a list of houses for rent. Mother was more interested in the garden than the house, and might have chosen a house much like some of the ones we would later live in: peeling paint, fewer flowers and shrubs than anybody else, a toilet out back, and all the garden space she could use. But she cared, too, that we children not feel too deprived after the collapse of our dreams of the spring and that we would all be comfortable in her first year in the seminary. She and Daddy quickly settled on half of a well-kept older house on North Stonewall Street. With a beautiful staircase in the impressive hall, bay windows, a wide front porch, and a porte-cochere on the side shaded by a magnolia tree, it made a good setting for the family of my daydreams who always moved with us. We lived and slept in two big rooms on the first floor heated by the grate in the living room and the wood stove in the kitchen; we used the two unheated rooms on the second floor only in very warm weather. The family of a preacher also going to Bethel lived in the other side of the house and shared the toilet under the stairs with us.

Having finally settled us after he and Mother found some second-hand furniture, Daddy was in a hurry, as always, to get away and start making a living. He left before the weekend was over. We all stood on the porch and waved good-bye as he moved the still new car out from under the porte-cochere. Trying to be funny about what I knew was a serious matter, I called after him, "Bring home the bacon, Daddy." "Have to catch the pigs first," he said, grinning, grim. I wished I hadn't said it.

A New Beginning

We had learned from our previous experience with new towns that some like strangers and some don't. Our first Sunday at Sunday School at the Cumberland Presbyterian church and our first days at school seemed to indicate that in McKenzie they would like us. Of course people at the college knew that Mother's aim was to be a preacher and not a school teacher as most people in town assumed. But in all the time we lived in McKenzie, none of us children ever mentioned to anyone outside the family Mother's ambition to be a minister.

That first year we lived within easy walking distance of Bethel and not more than a city block from the grammar school. Caroline passed into second grade her second week of school and John B. was in first. The big local crop, sweet potatoes, was twenty-five cents a bushel. When she got home early from Bethel each afternoon, Mother built up the fire in the kitchen stove and filled the oven with enough sweet potatoes to feed every child who appeared.

Somehow we had money to start off the school year. In those days long before schools in Tennessee and Kentucky thought of free school books, Mother cared intensely about clean new books for us. She took all of us to stand in line at Cannon's Drug Store which had the town concession for school books. I was the only student in seventh grade whose books were all new.

At least three piano teachers came visiting Mother to offer lessons to us children in the first few weeks. Mrs. Follinsbee, wife of one of the five or six doctors in town and the one we would see the most of, got there first. She offered to give four of us lessons for the price of two and to arrange for us to have first refusal on a piano she knew about. Mother agreed before she even asked Mary Elizabeth, who was home by then, and me to come meet her.

I was luckier with respect to "Expression," the art of telling stories or giving monologues that I had begun with Mrs. Forrest in Hiseville. My teacher was Mrs. Vance, the wife of an Education professor at Bethel, and mother of the Vance boys who ate many of

Mother's sweet potatoes. She was an attractive, but unusual looking woman whose long graying curls usually hung down her back. She had extensive experience as an actress in Cincinnati before she married Mr. Vance. She told Mother that "Expression" was no longer popular as it had been in her and Mother's day, but that she had a wide repertoire of pieces, both serious and funny, if I really liked memorizing. I could do minimal baby-sitting for her little daughter, Vivian, in exchange for lessons. Saturday by Saturday my memorized pieces increased, prose and poetry, funny and sad, suitable for giving at church, school, chapel, Lions' club, Garden Club, or Temperance meetings. As long as I lived in McKenzie, she and I were the two people who appeared most frequently to give readings as part of the entertainment at public meetings, I more often than she because I was more available.

Daddy was able to get home reasonably often during the fall. If he could not send money every week as he had hoped, a small check came in once a month from a gas well in Kentucky. We loved the little three-note whistle, "Swe-eet-heart" by which he signaled Mother to the door if he came after we were in bed Saturday night.

In the Theological Seminary at Bethel, Mother was the only woman in her classes year after year. Curiously, after Louisa Woosley's courageous struggle to be recognized as a minister, the ordination of several other women in the years 1910-1919, and the church's pioneering resolution on women in 1921, few women felt the Call, or chose to answer it in the 1920s and 1930s. Neither preachers nor laymen in the church as a whole, in contrast to her friends and neighbors in the Little Bend who had had the experience of Mrs. Woosley's evangelism, had truly accepted the idea of women preaching. Mother knew that, and no amount of prayer and determination could completely alleviate her anxiety and the pressure of being the only woman enrolled in the Seminary at the time.

At home she occasionally reported on the degree of respect, indifference, sometimes near insult, she received from one day to another. Some young preachers were awestruck by her ability in Greek which she began that first year, and Hebrew, the next. Some of the older teachers were respectful of her calling and willing to discuss at length the theological questions that concerned her. Other intelligent younger ones in her classes, like Morris Pepper, who became noted as a preacher and administrator in the church, and William Ingram, later her dissertation director (and president of the Seminary when it moved to Memphis), were impressed by her thoughtful questions and careful listening and remembered her as "in advance of her time." She often felt that others were impatient with her, wished to shake her off as soon as she could be dismissed, and were certain nothing would come of her theological education. She called them "Men!" Some of the women in the office and library seemed especially scornful. We children who had been the first to wish her calling away were entirely on her side within the confines of home. We thought of those who refused to give her their time as "scribes and pharisees" and her as "persecuted for righteousness' sake."

In considering her whole life, I believe that the three years from 1931 to 1934 Mother spent taking classes at Bethel, Depression and all, were among the happiest of her life. She was doing exactly what she wanted to do. For her, learning was not like cleanliness next to godliness; it was a part of godliness. However much she had loved her years at Hartford College, and reading Virgil as she rocked baby John's cradle at Teachers' College, all that was a preparation for the theological learning which she expected to teach her what she wanted to know most. She took as her own the four objectives of the Seminary as stated in the Annual Announcement: "To help the student to know God, to know God's word, to know how to teach God's word and his will; and to know and love the church."

We were never aware of exam time or term paper time as special periods. When it came to study, Mother simply did what was needed quietly and efficiently, often early in the morning before we were up. True, much of her time was still given to cooking, washing and ironing, gardening and canning. But as we children were older we were also more companionable. Mother was highly skilled at making good times for us at little expense and enjoyed them as much as we did. They were often centered on food. We pulled taffy all winter, made popcorn balls and snow ice cream during the infrequent snows. In summer there were watermelons at a nickel for a huge one and delicious desserts as each fruit came into season.

The promised piano was set in the kitchen on Stonewall Street. Caroline and I, who were the two that stuck with Mrs. Follinsbee's lessons, often practiced while Mother prepared supper. She herself sometimes sang hymns like "What a Friend We Have in Jesus" or "The Old Rugged Cross" with such concentrated vehemence that somebody had to do something really bad to get her attention, but there was also time for real conversation and sometimes we helped with her lessons.

One memorable course was "The Minister's Working Knowledge of the Bible." The text for the course was fifty small cards with Bible verses important for a minister to know printed on one side and the Bible reference on the other. Caroline or I stood beside her when she was rolling out biscuits (or earlier in the day, ironing) and read the Bible references. She responded with the words of the text. Then one of us read the words and she gave the references. We repeated again and again great passages from both the Old and New Testaments:

God is our refuge and strength, a very present help in trouble. Therefore we will not fear, though the earth be renewed, and though the mountains be carried into the midst of the sea. Ps. 46:1-2... *they that wait upon the Lord shall renew their strength; they shall mount up with wings as eagles; they shall run and not be weary; they shall walk and not faint.* Is. 40:31. We were sure that Mother's favorite was Deuteronomy 6:6-7: *And these words which I command thee this day shall be in thine ear; and thou shall teach them diligently unto thy children and shall talk of them when thou walkest by the way, and when thou liest down, and when thou risest up.* That passage kept us at family prayers and Bible reading.

When we were down to our last cent, we heard: *I have been young and now am old; yet have I not seen the righteous forsaken, nor his seed begging bread.* Ps. 37:25. I think we all really believed those words and felt assured that we were righteous enough to qualify.

Seventh Grade

The dress I wore my first day in seventh grade in McKenzie was sure to be good for conversation. It was made from the shiny yellow material called Peter Pan on which I had embroidered a hoop-skirted lady in a flower garden when I was in fourth grade, and it couldn't have been more different from the neat white-collared blouse and pleated skirt that Lloyd Allison wore. A Shaeffer fountain pen on a black ribbon hung around her neck. She was the student who rushed to give me paper to write down the books we would need after our teacher Miss Ophie pointed me to a seat in the front row. Harris Collier offered to loan me a pencil. I wouldn't decide for a year or so that he was the most attractive boy in the world, including movie stars, but I could see already that he was taller and had better skin and clothes and was nicer than you could usually expect boys to be.

As I accepted Lloyd's paper, I thought that if Annie Fellows Johnston, or any other children's author, were to walk into the room, she would choose Lloyd, the prettiest and best-dressed girl in the room, to be the heroine. She was blue-eyed and small, neither chubby nor skinny, and had light brown hair about the color of mine, which curved up from her shoulders. She also spoke with what I recognized as a refined southern accent. Even before I learned that Harris lived in the yellow brick house with white pillars on the corner of Magnolia and Stonewall and visited Lloyd in the home that replaced the plantation mansion that burned down, I associated both with the Old South.

Lloyd's best friend of many years had moved to Saint Louis during the summer and for almost a year I came close to taking her place with all the privileges that went with that position.

The first Saturday after school began she invited me to the red brick bungalow in which the family now lived. It was rather ordinary looking on the outside. I had visited homes in Bowling Green and Harlan that were as impressive or more so. But the spacious grounds were beautiful, and inside there was a difference, not just in the rugs and antiques that they had been able to save from their old home, but in manners and atmosphere. Her grandmother, "Miss Lola," had an elegant room of her own and before we settled down to play we went in to speak with her, as Lloyd's visitors always did, and to exclaim about the fine applique she was making for a quilt for Lloyd. A maid with a white cap and apron served lunch. It was set out on a starched damask table cloth with huge napkins. I was impressed that everybody had a glass of ice water and a choice of milk or iced tea.

I was often driven home with Lloyd after school and stood by as she completed her half hour of piano practice. Once or twice I went to the Beauty Parlor in town where she had her hair washed and set in the simple way that she wore it. She made sure that I was invited to join the Seven Secret Sisters in place of the friend who had moved away. At my first meeting we sat on a grassy part of the school grounds and promised that we would not date until we were out of seventh grade. I was welcomed to the Music Club sponsored by Lloyd's piano teacher, Mrs. Kelly, whom Mary Elizabeth and I wished Mother had signed us up with. I also became a Tenderfoot in the Girl Scouts after I read straight through the Girl Scout Handbook which Lloyd loaned to me.

The Tennessee fall was long and beautiful. Lloyd and I often joined a group of boys and girls who played "Hide and Seek" or "Signal" at each others' homes after school. Lloyd's family lived too far out of town for us to play at her house, but sometimes we played in the yard of the big yellow house that belonged to the Collier family and sometimes at the house of her friend, Rowena Everett, among others. Even needing to borrow the customary nickel or dime for ice cream or coca-cola at one of the drug stores downtown, after we were finished playing, did not spoil the fun. When it had been several days since Daddy sent us money, Mother and I took turns borrowing from one neighbor or another rather than ask Mary Elizabeth, the only member of the family with any money. Already sad from having to leave Grandmother and Granddad's farm to come to a strange town, she was unhappy that she was not being invited to play with my friends as she always had been in Kentucky.

Occasionally I attended the dance classes taught by the beau-

tiful red-haired Virginia Covington, recently home from being educated in the East. The others of the Seven Secret Sisters took tap
dancing and some took ballet. Lloyd was the only one who took both
"toe," which required toe shoes, and ballet which required only soft
shoes.

I knew that Mother thought I should invite Lloyd to our house,
especially after I had been to hers several times. She said so once or
twice but did not insist and kept putting sweet potatoes in the oven
for friends of the younger children. Reviewing every feature of our
house that bothered me, I worried about the problem for weeks. The
outside of the house was nice enough, and here at least we had an
inside toilet. But Granddad's old saying about three moves equaling
a fire certainly applied to our move to McKenzie. We had no rugs,
not even linoleum on the floor in the kitchen. Our living room was
furnished with a double bed in the bay window and two or three
cots. Since there were six of us when Daddy was at home, there was
a cot in the kitchen, too. The only other pieces of furniture were a
rocker and cane-bottomed chairs that were almost sat through.

I worried, too, about what games we would play, a question
that never came up when I was younger. But we seemed lacking in
all the equipment that other people had. Except for our old mother
cat and one runty kitten, we didn't even have the pets we brought to
McKenzie. The puppy Daddy had given us in Horse Cave had fallen
through the rails of the stair banister from the second floor and broken its neck, and Mother, tired of having the four kittens underfoot,
had tied them up in a stationery box and sent them off to be drowned
by a man who sold us wood. When one of the four, the ugly one that
belonged to Mary Elizabeth, came walking up the road a week later,
Mother came near weeping as she decided it could stay, "It wanted
so much to live."

Finally I suggested to Lloyd one day that she might come to
visit, but I was too tentative, and she quickly persuaded me that it
was nicer at her house, where she was the only child and there were
no younger children to bother us. A few days later, when Lloyd was
out of school for the day, I primed my nerve to invite Rowena Everett
whose home was not quite so intimidating as Lloyd's. She agreed
with an air of "Why in the world not?"

111

I was immediately sorry because I hadn't thought about what we were going to eat or what games we might play. I dreaded moving closer and closer to home with our armloads of books. Caroline and John B. were banging in and out of the screen door when we arrived. We managed to get past them and into the house and met Mother. She suggested that we put our books on the double bed in the alcove of the living room, rubbed her hands together a little to make sure they were clean, and offered Rowena her hand to shake. She apologized for not having anything to eat, "I don't suppose you girls would like some sweet potatoes?"

"No, thank you. We're not hungry."

Mother went into the kitchen to study until she was ready to start supper.

All the time I could see that Rowena was looking around. When Mother left, she said: "Where's your living room suite?"

I quickly put my answer together, "We left most of our things where we used to live. We came down here so Mother could go to school and we are just kind of camping out." To be certain I was not lying, I said: "But we never did have a living room suite."

She said that her family had always had a living room suite. Then she asked where the bathroom was. I was glad that I could show her the little room in the hall.

Meanwhile I still hadn't offered her a seat, but I asked her what she would like to play. Through the door to the kitchen she noticed the piano. I explained that mother wanted it there so that she could enjoy hearing Caroline and me practice when she was getting supper. Rowena laughed, "Let's play 'Chopsticks.'" She explained that it was not a game but a piano duet that she could teach me to play in no time.

"Rowena is going to teach me to play 'Chopsticks.' I said to Mother who was already sitting at the kitchen table, food and dishes pushed aside, absorbed in her studies. I pulled a chair up by the piano stool and Rowena showed me the notes. We hammered through it three or four times taking turns at the treble and the base.

Finally Mother raised her head, "Why don't you girls play something pretty?"

I realized that we were disturbing Mother, but was also hurt that she did not realize the special circumstances. We put down the piano lid and went into the living room, closing the door behind us. Rowena laughed and thumbed her nose toward the kitchen. Feeling cowardly, I laughed, too. Rowena moved toward our books: "Oh well, if there is nothing else to do, we might as well do homework." Pushing two of the straight chairs together and holding our tablets awkwardly on our knees, we began our arithmetic problems for the next day.

Although I continued to visit at both their houses, I never asked Rowena again to the house on Stonewall Street and I never invited Lloyd.

My failure to be hospitable did not seem to matter in the seventh grade. Mother managed Christmas allowances and I gave dime presents from Mr. Parnell's Variety Store to the Secret Sisters and two or three other Girl Scouts, probably the most presents I ever gave outside the family in my life. With that big circle of friends I enjoyed the pleasure of talking as Mother, my aunts, and their best friends did. We talked and talked in living rooms and on front porches and occasionally some of the crowd drifted to our front porch. We talked about how we got any visible scars, our worst whippings, past and present teachers, boys we couldn't stand, our favorite colors, foods, movie stars and our travels. Lloyd talked about the wonderful things she did with her cousins in Nashville. Rowena described her trips to New York and Washington. I told anecdotes about the places we used to live.

I had always liked school. In seventh grade I began to look forward to every day. In other years nobody except my parents and I had much cared whether I made good grades. Lloyd told me early that she had been "valedictorian" of her class every year since first grade, and that Harris Collier had been salutatorian every year through the fifth grade, after which he decided to quit trying and be more like the other boys. I had thought that words like "valedictorian" and "salutatorian" only applied to people like Mother and Daddy in high school, and had no idea whether I had ever been either. But month by month as our report cards came out, Lloyd and I stayed neck and neck, hardly able to wait until we showed our report cards to each other.

In Tennessee history I liked thinking about Indians and early settlers who had walked on the very ground under our feet. In my first exposure to English grammar, I was impressed that aside from what they said, words had names like "noun" and "adjective." I liked the way they fit together when we diagrammed sentences, something Mother had liked in school, too. One day we had parallel sentences: "He was an alumnus of Yale. She was an alumna of Vassar." It was plain that Vassar for women could be compared to Yale for men, and I remembered what my grandfather had said about "if he had it to do over."

I was still sick with asthma a good deal in those days when sick children stayed in bed. It could not have been easy for Mother to leave me alone in the big bed in the alcove of the living room when she went to classes. But we both knew that her classes were necessary and neither of us considered her not going. The minister's wife was usually at home in the apartment across the hall and I felt perfectly safe.

Mary Elizabeth and I were not getting along well and neither were she and Mother. After arrangements were made with Mrs. Follinsbee for all of us to take piano lessons, Mary Elizabeth refused to take any more lessons after her first, "I don't like the way she looks or talks or smells. And if I have to take lessons, I won't practice." Mrs. Follinsbee paid little attention to her appearance and did not have the nice cosmetic smell of the women we admired. John B. never took a single lesson. Mother decided that he was not ready for music lessons when he stayed in the hall outside his schoolroom until the lunch bell rang after his first-grade teacher excused him for his first lesson.

Caroline and John B., the younger children, had always been best friends and remained close all of their lives. Mary Elizabeth and I were the older sisters, for better or worse. For a few years after we moved to McKenzie the four of us split up another way. Once she learned to read, Caroline was always first in her class. Mary Elizabeth got good grades, but was not first, and so far as we knew, did not care. Caroline and I were taking advantage of our opportunity to be musical and receiving superior grades at school. Long after we were grown, John was still pointing to Caroline and me, "Those are your two valedictorians."

Once in a discussion about the Ten Commandments Mother explained that "Thou shalt have no other gods before me" and "Thou shalt not make unto thee any graven image" referred to false gods other than Baal. We caught on quickly. Mary Elizabeth said to me: "That's your friends in the seventh grade, Lloyd and them." I said back, "Well, how about your chickens at Grandmother's and the money you made?"

The end of school would seem to have been triumphant, but I felt that I paid dearly in terms of my friendship with Lloyd. Winning second place in the McDowell Club's piano contest was all right; Lloyd was not much interested in piano. As much as I liked to win, however, I was dismayed by winning first place in the WCTU (Women's Christian Temperance Union) essay contest for seventh graders. The contest judges described my essay, "Why a Good Writer Should Not Drink," as "a little more original" than Lloyd's "Why a Good Gym Teacher Should Not Drink." The award of a dollar bill for first place seemed insignificant in comparison with Lloyd's hurt when the WCTU woman officer made the announcement to our seventh grade class a few days before the end of school for the summer. Lloyd pretended she did not care when I was named "valedictorian" and she "salutatorian" on the last day of classes.

With summer vacation after seventh grade, Lloyd and I no longer saw each other regularly at school and the Millers did not have a telephone. By fall when we entered eighth grade, my family had moved to a house that was not on Lloyd's route to school. She had a big wiener roast during the fall to which she asked every one in the class. Mrs. Allison drove by to pick me up at the new address and I went to the roast. The next time somebody had a party to which I was invited, I had asthma. I was sick for the next party, too. Rowena came to visit me after one of those parties—it was easier to have company when I was sick—and told me about the wild things, like kissing games, that had gone on. Two missed parties, however, and suddenly everybody had grown up without me. When I got back to school, the former Seven Secret Sisters had broken up and some of the girls had begun dating.

Hard Times

The first time Daddy came home after we moved to McKenzie, I was sick with asthma. I hadn't been able to stop wheezing the day before after chasing with my friends to town to get ice cream cones and had spent most of the night propped up on pillows trying to breathe. Mother and I walked to town to see Dr. Williams, the happy-spirited community leader who was said to be the most popular doctor in town. He gave me a shot of adrenalin and a prescription for ephedrine, which could be bought, three capsules for a quarter, at Phelps Drug Store. After the walk home, I was still feeling cold, sweaty and wheezy and not very well when Daddy drove up into the side yard.

Caroline and John B. came in from their play, "We can't play now. Our Daddy's come home." After he had eaten, at the late hour, we sat in a circle around him, just looking at him for a minute or two and glad that he was safe at home again. I was over my asthma just like magic.

That was the day he told us some of our favorite stories. One was about the time Uncle Bob took longer than his turn bent over on the floor slapping the things he wanted in the Sears, Roebuck catalogue, and Daddy bit him on the bottom. Crippled Grandma Susie had Daddy reach the switch off the mantel and whipped them both. Daddy got a whipping another time when he stumbled over a stick of stove wood and broke every dish in the dishpan full of dishes he was carrying. Because he was trying to help we didn't think that whipping was fair.

When he was older Uncle Bob always took his dog named "Beloved Precious" to town with him. He liked speaking to the dog softly if a pretty girl came by: "Here Beloved Precious, here Beloved Precious." However she reacted, he could always say, "I was just calling my dog."

We never tired of hearing how Grandfather Miller knelt on a rattlesnake in a cotton field on one of those trips south. The sons slashed and sucked the bite as you read about in books and managed

117

to get him home alive in the wagon. His hair turned white, but he lived another ten years.

Usually Daddy came home on Saturday nights after we were all in bed in that front room where we all slept on Stonewall Street. I could hear his car drive up, then his little three-note whistle "Swe-eet-heart." Mother was at the front door, turning the key in the lock and unlatching the screen door almost as soon as he was on the porch: "Why, darling, I just felt like you would come this weekend."

We never saw the Sunday newspaper except when he came home and brought it with him. He liked to read it as it came fresh from the newsstand. We children didn't touch it until Sunday morning when we came home from Sunday School and church. Those old-fashioned comic strips were as much a part of our life with Daddy as his own stories: Mutt and Jeff, Maggie and Jiggs, Gasoline Alley, Little Orphan Annie and Popeye. Daddy was short like Mutt, but skinny like Jeff. He occasionally made a joke of pretending that Mother was "highbrow Maggie," always bullying him, and he was "lowbrow Jiggs" with the hole in his sock, and he would wave his toe through the hole to prove it. Mother was sure that the whole cartoon was against women, but was somehow flattered at being cast as "highbrow Maggie." Daddy had the cowlick of the Gasoline Alley characters, and we all dreamed of their nice middle-class life. Or if we could not have that, how about a Daddy Warbucks who would treat all four of us the way Daddy Warbucks treated Little Orphan Annie?

I certainly did not always get well because Daddy had come home. Sometimes it was nice to be sick when he was there and I did not have to go to church Sunday morning. I lay in the big bed and the two of us would interrupt our reading of either the paper or books to talk now and then.

Lloyd and the seventh grade crowd had helped to replace my love of *The Little Colonel* with the more up-to-date *Outdoor Girls* and *Nancy Drew*. But I had also begun going on Friday afternoons to the McKenzie Library on the top of Cannon's Drug Store and discovered many books by popular writers of Daddy's growing-up years: *The Girl of the Limberlost* and *Freckles* by Gene Stratton

Porter, *The Little Shepherd of Kingdom Come* by John Fox, Jr., and some by Harold Bell Wright. Eventually I got hold of *David Copperfield* and *Huckleberry Finn* which were special favorites of his and remained important to me for the rest of my life. We also talked about American history and I learned to love and revere Thomas Jefferson and Abraham Lincoln.

One particular weekend in seventh grade I was not happy when Daddy came home. Lloyd and I both received A's and A minuses in every other subject, but up until late January we both got C's for penmanship. We were using our fingers instead of our arms to create the Palmer Method ovals and push and pulls which Miss Ophie was trying to teach us. Then suddenly one Friday afternoon when I had stayed after school to practice, the feeling for writing with my arm came to me. From a teachers' magazine I traced out a profile of Abraham Lincoln and filled it in with perfect ovals. When Daddy came home that weekend, I showed it to him. I was pleased because I knew the ovals were right and I could include it in the penmanship notebook which was due Monday; he was pleased because, even made in ovals, you could tell it was Lincoln. Monday morning as I started to school, he asked me for the picture to show to his friends on the road. I knew I couldn't reproduce the piece in time to hand it in with my notebook; I shook my head, "I can't." Lloyd soon learned to write with her arm and made an A in penmanship at the end of February. The one extra A I made in penmanship may have made the difference in the comparison of our grades that year. I never forgot that I had denied Daddy one of the few things for which he ever asked me.

Before summer Daddy had to sell the new car we had been so proud of and he tried selling one product and then another. One was an energy-saving device for gas stoves that he sold door to door. He told us stories about the women he sold to and was proud of any sales, but he did not make much money, and the checks from the Kentucky gas well became less regular and then stopped altogether. He came home by bus or on one of the two train lines that crossed in McKenzie. He usually came at night because he hated to be seen walking down the street with the awkward big box which he needed for whatever he was selling.

Once during the summer, he was stranded in Huntingdon, the county seat of Carroll County from which no trains or buses ran to McKenzie. I don't know whether he tried to hitchhike, but in any case he was not offered any rides and he walked the entire fifteen miles. Mother did not cry when she secretly showed me his shoes with holes worn through the soles and told me about his blistered feet. But her face was deeply serious. This was not a time when she could blame him for not being able "to make a go of it." While she kept praying that he would bring or send home more money, the decision to leave the comparatively good-paying teaching job in Hiseville and follow the oil bubble had been her decision as well as his.

After that period of several months without a car, he managed to get a second-hand car and after that another. He was never without a car again, but his expenses on the road took most of the money he made. During the five years from the time we moved to McKenzie in 1931 until his disappearance in 1936, he came and went and gave us a few glimpses of the life he was living away from us: "the friends on the road"; the housewives whose gas stoves he adjusted; newspapers on an eastern Kentucky hotel bed to keep him a little less cold. There was also the hungry man to whom he gave a quarter at the door of a small restaurant. We were ashamed of Mother when she protested that "we could have used that quarter so well"; it didn't seem like her. Occasionally he brought us news of neighbors and acquaintances in the places where we had formerly lived, and he made one or two visits to see Grandmother and Granddad and Anna and her family after they moved back to the farm. He reported that Granddad, now in his seventies, was enjoying a battery-run radio for the first time. He made at least one trip to visit the folks in Texas. But he never stayed long anywhere. Sometimes at home he sat for what seemed like hours with his elbows on his knees and his face clasped in his hands.

Before our first summer was over, Mother found a gray weather-beaten old house with a large garden that backed up to the Bethel campus. We moved from Stonewall Street to that house on the dirt road called Laurel Street. Going back to an outdoor toilet made us feel poor and we did not yet know about the bedbugs.

I continued to have asthma and too many of the family's few quarters went for the three ephedrine tablets that would help me to breathe for three nights. A dollar would have replaced John B.'s torn Lindbergh cap held together with a safety pin all winter the year he was in second grade. To counterbalance my asthma and the sense of being poor was whatever was happening with my hormones as a 12-year-old and the interest of eighth grade. We were preparing for the county examinations that all eighth graders had to take before they went into high school. That was also the year of the school's decision to assign different teachers to different subjects in the last two years of grammar school. During the Depression years when jobs everywhere were scarce, the conscientious McKenzie School Board snapped up for teaching positions the local young people who had been "first" in high school and at Bethel College. Our history teacher, Miss Aileen, the daughter of a Bethel professor, was a Civil War enthusiast. Our English teacher, Miss Willard, asked us to write our own "Christmas Carol" using Dickens as a model. I cast Daddy in the role of Bob Cratchit and wrote a story of more than twenty pages.

Not local was our homeroom teacher Brother Rose, a red-haired Baptist minister, who was principal of the grammar school as well as the eighth-grade arithmetic and geography teacher. He never actually used the wooden paddle laid out on the desk in front of him when a lower grade boy was "sent to the principal," but we did have to live through some miserable quarter hours of cross-examination. We also became familiar with Brother Rose's anthology of Baptist preacher jokes. But he cared deeply about educating us as well as keeping order and entertaining us. If businessmen were still jumping out of windows in the large cities in the fall of 1932, in McKenzie some families were losing their homes, fathers were losing and changing jobs and losing their businesses, women were busy in ways they had never been before. Rowena's family moved almost as often as we did. Lloyd's mother worked most evenings at the box office of the family's movie theatre and traded movie tickets for things like her and Lloyd's trips to the beauty parlor. Of course we did not talk about these things in class as we did not in private. Most people in town seemed to think the election of 1932 was primarily about making alcohol legal again. Certainly opposed to drinking himself, Brother Rose tried to make us see that there were other things to be considered besides the repeal of the eighteenth amendment.

Mother thought of herself as a Republican like Granddad and was inclined to favor Mr. Hoover after hearing him inaugurated on the Chaplin school radio. Once you were president, you were "somebody," and therefore interesting, but she had never taken politics very seriously, had seen the electoral process as a rather trivial competition, somewhat like baseball, that interested men in their leisure time. Much as she hated liquor, however, she became convinced with Daddy in the election of 1932 that some kind of change was necessary. I have found it sad to remember that, given the complications of poll tax and registration in a new town, it is unlikely that either voted the year of Roosevelt's first election.

About the time Roosevelt was inaugurated as President in 1933—and even people who did not have any money were shocked by the closure of the banks—Mother was planning her garden on Laurel Street. Both before school closed for the summer and afterward, she and we four children picked strawberries from a flat field across the dirt road that ran in front of our house. Even at two cents a quart, each girl made enough money for a length of dress material, and John B. bought a new pair of overalls.

The owner's daughter, home from her music studies in some northern city, sometimes picked along with us. One day Mother brought her into the house for a drink of water. She showed her the family pictures including the graduation picture from Bowling Green and told her about the deaths of her two sisters and Uncle Henry. Since they had become that intimate, Mother mentioned that I had begun to menstruate. Humiliated by my mother's talking about "that," I cried and stayed out of the strawberry field when the woman appeared again.

Mother told me that Daddy was aware that we girls would soon begin menstruating and that he hoped she would be prepared with nice bought sanitary napkins and elastic belts when the time came. Momentarily I was aware that my parents considered all this their business as well as mine. But both Mother and I realized that, with the little money we had, there was no question of monthly trips to the drug store for the familiar shaped boxes "other girls" were beginning to pick up.

Before our second summer in McKenzie was over, Mother began to accept hand-outs of canned milk and flour from the Red Cross. That, Mary Elizabeth and I felt, was more humiliating than bed bugs. Mrs. Thorne came into our lives at an important time.

A Joyful Giver

Mother, who was always ready to join another Bible class, became a member of Mrs. Eula Thorne's group of four or five women Bible readers soon after we moved to that miserable house on Laurel Street. She talked about Mrs. Thorne as the weeks went by. "Oh, she's a wonderful woman. She knows more about the Bible than most of those men over at Bethel." We occasionally caught a glimpse of Mrs. Thorne, her white scarf flying, when she drove Mother home. But it was well into the next summer before Mother asked her to supper. She could see that Mary Elizabeth and I were surprised. We had had no company above Caroline's and John B.'s age for a meal since we came to McKenzie. "You'll see. She'll take us like we are."

We were glad for the next door neighbors, in a house as rundown and unpainted as ours, to see Mrs. Thorne's green Pontiac parked in front of our house; some friends in Middle Tennessee had given it to her when she wrecked her old car. As she came up the rickety steps, Mrs. Thorne was dressed all in white as she always was, even white shoes at any time of year. If anybody asked her why, she said that it was so she would be ready to meet "my angel"—that was Brother Thorne—when she got to heaven.

People liked to talk about her, and we had heard much before she appeared at our house. She and the Reverend William Thorne came to live in McKenzie in the early 1900s, and he spent twenty years as a home missionary to several rural Presbyterian churches in West Tennessee. When he died in 1925, he left Mrs. Thorne their home with its big lot and garden on the corner of Spruce and Magnolia Streets and, according to town legend, $10,000 in cash. After we got to know her, she frequently told us girls that she had married a man who was her superior "spiritually, mentally, and physically" and urged us to do the same.

Now almost before the Depression had really begun, she had spent all the money she had inherited. In the period before any kind of government help was available, she was always finding families who needed food or fuel, children with eyes to uncross, young people with appendixes to remove, women who needed winter coats. Black, white, sharecropper, middle class, she didn't turn anyone away. The orphan boy whom she helped set up in the beauty parlor business became a substantial citizen and member of the Lions' Club. But most of the people would not "amount to much" or at least that is what her acquaintances said. They were the tenants and sharecroppers who had moved into town when they could no longer make a living in the country. Already in the twenties cotton and corn had been raised too long on the red hills of West Tennessee. Land owners were desperate, too, and there was less and less room for their tenants. Every year families were moving from the country to the bunch of little rundown shacks on the road to Memphis called Brawnertown. If the immigrants were hoping there would be somebody like Mrs. Thorne, there was. Eventually she put a mortgage on her house and ran up bills at the several family grocery stores in town for whoever needed food, until the grocers would give her no more credit. Finally, she could give only the dollar at a time that her old friends in Middle Tennessee frequently enclosed in their letters. If she received a dollar in the morning, she tried to give it away before night, believing that made it more likely she would receive another dollar the next day.

Still she always looked nice, which mattered to Mary Elizabeth and me. Except for her protruding front teeth which some people said made her look like Eleanor Roosevelt, she had a model's features and carried herself like a queen who had to get somewhere in a hurry. She kept herself busy from morning to night visiting the old and sick in both town and country and making appearances at rural churches and schools, and at the black Webb High School where she led a weekly chapel program. She also belonged to the Music, Book, and Garden clubs like the women in town we called "society ladies."

An eccentricity of a different order from her extravagant charity was her extravagant speech. Her talk sometimes seemed to consist of a few connectives between words like "lovely," "beautiful," "glorious" and "ex-*quis*-ite"(with the accent on the second syllable).

126

That first night at supper after she had thanked the Lord for "these darling children," and we had eaten our "ex-*quis*-ite" supper of garden vegetables, buttermilk, biscuits, and strawberry jam, she suggested that we all go to the picture show: "A dollar came in the mail this morning."

My heart leapt. *State Fair*, a film based on a novel I loved, with my favorite movie star, Janet Gaynor, was playing at Lloyd's parents' theater. Now that I was twelve, I would have to pay a quarter rather than a dime for admission and had doubted that I would ever see it. I certainly had never hoped that Mother would be able to see it. Not unexpectedly, she said that she could not take time from her studies and asked Mrs. Thorne: "Why don't you take U.T. and Mary Elizabeth and I'll stay home with the little ones?"

Caroline and John B. began to cry. Mary Elizabeth said, "Come on, Mother. Mrs. Thorne wants to give us a present." Mother was not comfortable. She thought picture shows were luxuries for other people. But finally she consented.

After the film was over, the six of us spilled out of the theater. Mother exclaimed loud enough for anybody to hear, "Who-oo, the farm was never like that. They will try to make people believe anything." "But wasn't it beautiful?" said Mrs. Thorne. I agreed. The picture of the boy and girl at the State Fair swinging out into the night on the ferris wheel would stay with me for a long time. How many different boys I would dream onto that ferris wheel!

Before time came for school to open, a house owned by Aunt Grace Bridges, Mother's best friend in the Bible class, became empty on Spruce Street around the corner from Mrs. Thorne's house on Magnolia. Aunt Grace (the only friend in McKenzie we called "Aunt") lived on Spruce, too, and persuaded Mother that we ought to be her and Mrs. Thorne's neighbors. Before school started in September we moved to the house which we liked best of the five places we lived in McKenzie.

The two and a half years there were crucial for all of us. I went from freshman year in high school to junior, Mary Elizabeth from sixth grade to eighth, and Caroline and John B. to fourth and fifth. Mother finished her class work at the seminary and began work on the required dissertation. We liked our neighbors and they liked us. The men looked up to Mother for the wonderful gardens she grew. Never mind that she was still going to school at an age when most women would be expecting grandchildren. The neighbor women brought me lunches and other treats when I was at home sick in bed with asthma.

All of us spent much time at the flower and plant decorated house Mrs. Thorne prided herself on never locking. And we all rode around in her car. Caroline and John sometimes rode into the country with her when she went to hand out gospels and church papers at farm houses. If she was not in a hurry, she would stop the car to let them wade in a creek by the side of the road or poke grass through a fence to a favorite horse. Mary Elizabeth sometimes mopped and dusted Mrs. Thorne's rooms, and Mrs. Thorne always gave her a nickel or a dime. Before long she had a regular job with the tenant who lived in the other part of the house. I spent hours on Mrs. Thorne's living room couch reading the novels which were exchanged among the Englenook Book Club ladies. It was nice to be quiet in the pretty, light room and read recently bought clean new books like Willa Cather's *Shadows on the Rock*, Pearl Buck's *The Good Earth*, and many others.

I liked arranging flowers, from Mrs. Thorne's garden as well as those we brought in from the fields. It was hardly believable that wild flowers had names like "Queen Anne's Lace"!

Both Mary Elizabeth and I liked the possibility of seeing the dark haired, good-looking young man whom Mrs. Thorne thought of as a son. He had a cleft in his chin like Clark Gable's. She had kept an eye on him and his mute mother since he was a small boy. Recently she had helped them to move to half a house nearby on Magnolia Street. When not at school or football practice or on dates in Mrs. Thorne's car with various girls said to be the nicest in town, he was often around the house. We sniffed his shaving lotion and flirted a little. He was the first boy I ever kissed—the summer after my first year in college when I came home determined to be kissed before fall.

My sister Caroline says that she can still repeat Psalms 1, 8, 24 and 27 from having learned them with Mrs. Thorne. I also learned 19, 46, and 91. The first year on Spruce Street I rode out into the country with Mrs. Thorne to pick up a friend who otherwise would not have been able to go to high school since Tennessee had no school buses in those days. As she drove, she said aloud and I repeated after her one of the Psalms and, eventually, the Beatitudes and the 13th chapter of First Corinthians. The following summer I took regular Bible lessons with Mrs. Thorne in her garden. A "lesson" meant that I read aloud a chapter at a time. She would occasionally correct the pronunciation of a place name, peering at me over her glasses as she did any necessary mending. (Neither she nor Mother knit or crocheted—Mother said that was not work the Lord had for her and Mrs. Thorne to do.) She insisted that I read all the genealogies and the *begats, cubits*, and *shekels* because they were all holy and all had their point.

After one of my first lessons, several children who were to have a lesson after me came pushing through the garden gate. They were barefoot and ragged with sores and mosquito bites wherever you looked. As I waved good-bye and closed the gate, I could hear they were working on the eighth Psalm, *What is man that thou art mindful of him?...Thou hast made him a little lower than the angels.*

I was sometimes embarrassed when Mrs. Thorne asked the young men in the filling stations where she bought a dollar's worth of gas whether they were saved. They always answered seriously, "I aim to be," "I hope so," or very solemnly, "No'm." "Well, God loves you and don't you forget it," she would say as she held out her dollar bill.

Mrs. Thorne was one of the people who sponsored my career as an elocutionist. Working with Mrs. Vance I had begun to accumulate a considerable repertoire and was taking her place when she began to be tired of public readings. My temperance readings were perfect for the WCTU (the Women's Christian Temperance Union) and for rural churches, and I read at the various clubs to which Mrs. Thorne belonged. Once I gave a reading at her weekly chapel program at Webb High, the school for Negro children. The two of us carefully selected the piece I was to give. No, not one of the temperance pieces, and none of the funny pieces about "colored people." We decided to use "Sister in the Medicine Closet," the monologue of a little girl as she removes various medicines from the bathroom shelves and doses her little brother.

The principal, Professor Seats, met us at the door of Webb High. With his starched collar, vest, and watch chain, he looked the way Mother liked men to look, and as well as I can remember was the first black man I ever saw in a suit on a weekday. "Is this the young lady who is going to give us the reading?" As we walked through the hall to the auditorium, I was amazed by the many ways the "colored" school resembled the white schools I had attended: the same construction paper tulips and bunnies for Easter pasted on the school windows, the same pictures of Lincoln and of Washington crossing the Delaware hung on the classroom walls, the same yellow song books laid out on every other seat in the auditorium. Mrs. Thorne and I sat on the stage beside Professor Seats and I had plenty of time to look at the little sea of nearly white to tan and dark brown faces, ranging from the first-graders in the front row to the high schoolers at the back. I was sure that I must have seen many of them before and should know a few, but no one looked familiar in the context of that auditorium. Mrs. Thorne read and talked about one of our favorite psalms. Then I was called on.

I was on the verge of dismay when no laughter came with the first four or five lines of "Sister in the Medicine Closet" as there always was when I gave it to white audiences. Did these children know what a medicine closet was? Few of them had bathrooms. Did they feel they shouldn't laugh when a white girl was giving a speech? But soon they began to catch on: "Castor oil is terrible for children." With one laugh, there were more, and by the end when I ran to the back of the stage wailing after my imaginary spanking and rubbing my backside, the laughter and clapping were pleasantly vociferous. Mrs. Thorne had proposed that I omit "that little gesture at the end," but in my eagerness to hold my audience I didn't dare risk it. Years later when one black woman or another met Mother on the street, she would ask her, "Is your girl the one that gave the speech to the children's school?"

As important as she was to all of us children, Mrs. Thorne may have been most important to Mother. About the time we moved to Spruce Street, Mother began to teach the "Young Adults" Sunday School class at the Cumberland Presbyterian church. The group included some of the student preachers at the college and their wives as well as some Bethel faculty wives. Early Sunday morning before church, Mother regularly spent an hour with Mrs. Thorne to catch "that spiritual height." She gave her whole heart and good mind to the class for several years and was often pronounced "the best Sunday School teacher" they ever had.

Mother also began going out occasionally with Mrs. Thorne to visit some of her rural families and the families in Brawnertown. She had always thought of herself as open to people "of all sorts and conditions," but in the farm country in which she grew up, there was a deep prejudice against the relatively few "down and out." The men were thought of as "just too lazy to work," and their families were outcasts. Under Mrs. Thorne's tutelage and her own life in McKenzie, Mother found new depths of sympathy in herself and began to see the worth of the poorest. The Sunday School class she started in Brawnertown on Sunday afternoons was as much of a success as her morning class at the Cumberland Presbyterian Church.

We were still living on Spruce Street when Mrs. Thorne had her second wreck. It was at one of the numerous flat railroad crossings in town, in the second car given her by her friends in Middle Tennessee. She had not been hurt at the first wreck which had occurred before we came to McKenzie, but the second time, though no bones were broken and she did not receive any bad cuts, she had to stay at home in bed for two or three weeks afterward. With the other neighbors who wanted to help I spent several hours of many days at her bedside. Haunted by the fear that she might die, I had plenty of time to be angry with the women who, loving her as they obviously did, still enjoyed scolding about her differences from other people: "Can you imagine? Someone not having enough sense to stop at a crossing when a train is coming? And a second time, too?"

The Way We Lived

As Daddy sent less and less money home, Mother became more ingenious about contriving ways to stretch what he sent as far as it would go. Any money had to go first for rent, and we moved five times during our first six years in McKenzie though the only move we made merely to save on rent was the one from Stonewall Street to Laurel.

We lived upstairs, downstairs, practically at the town square with three churches less than a block away, out on the edge of town, on main streets, and side streets. All were heated by a fireplace or a stove in the living room with a wood and coal burning stove in the kitchen. On Stonewall Street and at Miss Gerta's on Church Street we had indoor toilets (outside privies at the other three), and at Miss Gerta's a bathtub with hot water furnished by her hot water heater, but even there as in every other place, the wooden sink in the kitchen had only a cold-water tap.

Since McKenzie had town water, we never had to carry water from a well. But it was as important to pay the monthly water bill of $1 or $1.50 as to pay the rent. Next to rent and water, money for wood or for wood and coal mattered most. A whole group of desperate, hungry white men seemed to survive by the dollar bills that were the price for a load of wood, cut from we never knew where. The wood always came in chunks too big to go into the kitchen stove. Mary Elizabeth sometimes chopped the chunks to make them fit, and John B. chopped as he got older, but meal preparation for Mother often began with an ax. Whether the wood was dry or green was the difference between a warm efficient kitchen and a cold smoky one. Mother liked to brag that she could judge a man's character by looking into his face, but we knew that she could never tell whether his wood was wet or dry, no matter what he promised. To stretch the good luck of a dry load, the next dollar that came into her hands purchased another load, sure to be wet, which would make the dry load last longer.

When we moved to Spruce Street, Mother never had the utilities company turn on the electricity. With kerosene at fifteen cents a gallon, we saved maybe $1.50 a month by using a kerosene lamp for light. The electric iron brought from Kentucky gave out the first year and was never replaced. Mother ironed with black flat irons like those she had grown up with on the farm. Asking myself now why in my teens I wasn't doing my own ironing, I realize that Mother was touched by the "other people" complex. She might have encouraged me to master the equipment if she had not felt so apologetic about it. "Other people" had good ironing boards and electric irons, so naturally many other girls my age were beginning to do their ironing.

Mother's attitude toward the cooking was much the same as that toward the laundry. Each of us learned to make certain specialties—I, drop biscuits in my first year of high-school Home Economics, Mary Elizabeth, corn bread at Grandmother's. "Other people" had gas or electric ranges and nicely kept kitchen utensils. If we had had better things to work with, maybe the girls would have learned to be "real cooks." Mother and her sisters had learned to cook with no more modern equipment than we had, but they were both inferior and superior to us—inferior because they used inferior equipment, but superior enough to do things we couldn't do.

Mary Elizabeth loved learning many skills at Grandmother and Granddad's. Along with chopping wood and making a fire in the stove (she could milk a cow, too), she was proud of ironing her own clothes by the time she was eleven. When she was in sixth grade, Mother began to depend on her to get up early before school to help do the wash the way the family always had— outside with tubs and rub board, hung on the lines in the yard in all weathers. With that contribution to the family welfare Mother was reluctant to call on Mary Elizabeth for many other things that she was capable of doing, surely because I with my asthma was called on for so little. I was usually let off even from dish washing: "I wouldn't have that child get sick for anything." My sister could not believe that I was all that delicate: "Why can't U.T. do something?" I was suspicious that she thought I was being rewarded for making good grades at school and practicing the piano.

Without refrigeration we drank lots of buttermilk at ten cents a gallon and ate eggs at ten cents a dozen. Most of what we bought at the grocery store was to make something else—non-Red-Cross flour (I had to sift the worms out of the Red-Cross flour to make my first drop biscuits required by a Home Economics assignment), meal, and lard. Day-old grocery bread at half price was strictly saved for school lunch sandwiches. Caroline and John B. sometimes took their blackberry jam on biscuits to school, but not Mary Elizabeth and I. Our meat was an occasional ten-cent soup bone, strips of fat back to fry and make gravy, and liver and sausage when we knew a neighbor had killed hogs. A jar of peanut butter, the cheapest salad dressing, or a box of processed cheese always disappeared in a few hours, so they were bought only as luxuries to celebrate special occasions.

As I had anticipated on our first drive through town, we did run up small bills at all the small grocers, returned to one or another when we could pay a little on account, spent most of any money in hand at U-Tote'em, the cash grocery in town. I remember once being sent to U-Tote'em for three cents worth of salt. "How about a nickel's worth?" No, three cents was the cash Mother had.

Most important in feeding us was Mother's garden and her canning which was an extension of the gardening process. We had huge gardens at each of the five places we lived in McKenzie. After she found a neighbor with a horse and plow to break the ground in the spring, she was out at dawn in a pair of galoshes or rubbers to protect her feet from the dew—plowing with her little hand plow, raking, hoeing, and planting. The motions to make the plants grow came as near to prayer as prayer itself. While she believed that God was always with her, He made Himself most reassuringly present in the garden. In the morning silence, she did not need the protection of the hymns she sang in the kitchen.

Harvesting was work for late afternoon when the plants were dry and we were encouraged to help gather the food we ate. Mother felt a sensuous thrill in finding a big green pepper or a perfect to-mato, and she believed that we were sharing the thrill with her when she asked us to look for them. We could see what she meant about peppers and tomatoes, but green beans were a different matter. Mother's ardor for green beans was as great as her enthusiasm for blackberries. She canned hundreds of half gallons of green beans, tomatoes and blackberries, the tomatoes and green beans from the garden and the blackberries free along road sides and in uncultivated fields.

One staple we were never without was sugar. Mother liked sweet things herself, and she believed some kind of dessert made almost any meal palatable to children. We ate in cycles the dishes she could prepare from the food available— several weeks of fried apple pies which we might or might not eat again for several months, weeks of peach cobbler, of apple cobbler, of chess pies (a favorite delicacy made with eggs), of yellow cake with crushed strawberries on top. Sometimes a meal would be as many pieces of pie as we could eat and a glass of buttermilk. In the course of a week, we ate most of the foods necessary for good nutrition, but we never had to have all the nutrients at any one meal. Looking at the list above, I see how well we ate compared with the really deprived of the world. The skills that Mother had learned on the farm kept us almost luxuriously alive. This is not to say that Mother never heard complaints about what we ate: "Why do we always have the same thing?" "Why can't we have more light bread?" We knew not to complain about the lack of meat.

As for clothes, except for shoes, they were the last thing Mother thought of spending money on. Mostly we depended on hand-me-downs. In the girls' fiction I read, the less well-off children and youth resented clothes from rich relatives or "the missionary barrel." Even Mary Elizabeth, who probably suffered more than Caroline and I did from not having store-bought clothes, liked clothes given to us by people we liked. I remember feeling almost glamorous in dresses that my Expression teacher gave me and those of Louise Adams, "Miss McKenzie" year after year in the town's beauty pageant.

During our first years in McKenzie, jobs for children like picking strawberries did not come along often. There were more possibilities as we got older. Along with working for Mrs. Thorne's tenant, Mary Elizabeth was a favorite with both Mr. Grady Snead the mailman and Mr. Rucker the milkman, who each drove a horse. On Saturdays, and whenever she wasn't at the farm in the summer, they often gave her a nickel or dime to ride with them and climb down from their vehicles with mail or a small milk order.

Like all of us, John B. was a dreamer and after he learned to read was tempted by magazine ads promising big money for the sale of seeds, salves, or Christmas cards. Aunt Grace or Mrs. Thorne could usually be induced to take one or two samples, but then he had to pay the return postage on the cans of salve or the boxes of Christmas cards that had not sold. He was luckier when he discovered that he could sell scrap iron, not for much money, but enough to keep him and his red wagon constantly on the prowl.

By the time we were in high school, baby-sitting was the most profitable job for both Mary Elizabeth and me, especially as the word "baby-sitter" began to be used. We could make a quarter for a long evening, or a dollar for a weekend when the family went out of town, and then we became friends of the family. One of my families gave me my first permanent.

One way and another, Mother, or we by our own efforts, managed money for an occasional movie and for season tickets to the high school football games. When we began to have favorite movie stars, Mother tried to make sure that we got to their movies. High points for me were Greta Garbo in *Queen Christina* and *Anna Karenina*, Katherine Hepburn in *Little Women* and *The Little Minister*, and Ronald Colman in *Tale of Two Cities*. We saw films with Will Rogers, Marie Dressler, and Shirley Temple. I can remember that it rained the Saturday afternoon that *Little Women* was on. Mother was hesitant about letting me go out in the rain. She said: "Would you rather go and take the chance of being sick or stay home and be well?" I took the chance and promptly got asthma after seeing the Katherine Hepburn film. I never regretted the choice.

Neighbors

We called Aunt Grace Bridges "Aunt" because she was Mother's special friend and had insisted that we move near her on Spruce Street. She was a pretty woman in her late thirties with yellow ringlets and teeth that showed lots of gold when she smiled. The tragedy of her life was that she had never had any children of her own. Each of us four children just suited her and her husband, Uncle John, in one way or another. The younger children often appeared at feeding time for Uncle John's hunting dogs to help throw the corn bread that Aunt Grace baked in huge pans across the fence to the dogs' yard. Aunt Grace and I had in common the *Cosmopolitan* and *Good Housekeeping* magazines which she laid out for me on the day they arrived.

We both agreed that some of the magazine stories with nude bathing and babies born out of wedlock were shocking. But neither in the stories nor in the illustrations were there people who resembled in the least the scary-looking men and wretched buttermilk-complexioned women who began coming and going from the tenant house at the end of Spruce Street about a year after we moved there.

One Saturday morning when I was visiting Aunt Grace to return some borrowed magazines, she suddenly interrupted our talk to run to a front window and pulled aside the curtain. She pointed to two men walking along the road: "There they are. They are going to visit those women." One man was carrying a side of bacon by its wire hook and the other a sack of what must have been flour or meal. I recognized them as the worn sharecropper types we sometimes saw in town on Saturday afternoons. One expected the scraggly beards, but I had never noticed men quite so ragged and dirty. Aunt Grace knew about the family of women and children who had moved into the tenant house. These and other men made regular visits.

The arrival of the Brundy women on the street was a shock to all the neighbors. Each Saturday morning curtains were pulled back when you could see a man or two going by. They were usually afoot, though occasionally one passed by in a wagon pulled by a mule. Aunt Sis and Aunt Patia, older neighbors who brought me sick trays when I had asthma, shook their heads and clucked their tongues. Aunt Grace could add the most details. Nobody could remember who had lived in the house last. Whoever these people were, they belonged to the most derelict element from the country.

When she found out about the family, Mother did not respond to the gossip with the same thrill of horror as the other neighbors. She was particularly concerned with the women, "Why the poor things. We can't let a thing like that go on, and the children ought to be in school." Aunt Grace who had come from the country herself said, "There's nothing you can do for people like that." Mother knew about "no account" people, especially no account men, but these people right on the street were "neighbors," people the Bible recognized as especially precious.

"Why, of course, darling," Mrs. Thorne instantly agreed when Mother proposed that the two of them make a visit to the Brundys. A few days later she picked up Mother in her car and the two of them with their Bibles drove to the field in which the house stood—you couldn't call it a "front yard." There was a little scrabbling and scratching before the door on the leaning porch opened. The woman whom they soon learned was old Mrs. Brundy answered the knock and opened the door a crack. Mrs. Thorne quickly introduced herself and Mother, "I am Mrs. Thorne and this is Mrs. Miller. We've come to talk to you about your Bibles."

Old Mrs. Brundy threw the door wide open: "Why, honey, come right in here. I just love to hear about the Bible. I can't hear enough about it." She called Rhoda, the younger woman who was either her daughter or daughter-in-law, we were never sure which, to come into the room. Rhoda and one child after another began to appear. Clothes piled on two kitchen chairs were removed to the end of the bed and the chairs offered to the guests. Rhoda, looking like one of the women I would recognize later in Margaret Bourke White's or Walker Evans' photographs, was gray-faced, tired, and obviously pregnant. She sat on the bed with a two-year-old in her lap and another little girl beside her. There was a girl about twelve and a ten-year-old boy. The children were all barefoot in November.

Mother took the four-year-old on her lap.

"Honey, don't pick her up," said the older woman. "I know she's dirty." With the child's head under her chin, Mother wondered how long it had been since her hair had been washed, but she knew that children liked to be held, and settled the little girl with her arms around her.

Mrs. Thorne perched her glasses on the end of her nose. She selected the passage from the New Testament about Jesus suffering the little children to come, told them that we are all little children. Then she suggested that they pray. The older woman said, "Honey, you go ahead."

Mrs. Thorne prayed as she would have prayed for any family. "Lord, bless these dear children and this young mother." Mother expressed her hopes, "May this be a new day in the life of this family."

When the praying was over the two asked practical questions: "Are the children in school? .... Do you have enough to eat?"

Mother looked at Rhoda and commented on her condition, "Honey, I can see you are going to have a little baby. Is a doctor looking after you?"

When asked about food they said they had plenty, but the children were out of school because they didn't have clothes. "For another thing," Rhoda said that they were from the country and town seemed strange. She didn't usually bother about a doctor until she just had to have him.

After that Mother and Mrs. Thorne made regular visits. They chose not to talk about the men at first. But they always took their Bibles and prayed. Mother soon learned the names of all the children and their ages and would approach acquaintances with children their age for clothes to give them.

One very cold day Mother confronted a man hanging around the place when there was no wood for the stove, "The next time I come here, I want to see a big load of wood out back." The next week the man wasn't there, but the wood was. The room they sat in seemed a little more orderly; clothes hung on hooks, the quilt spread out smoothly on the bed. But the children still had not had their hair washed and they did not have shoes.

Mother had not been to the Red Cross office in some time, but she was glad to inquire about shoes for the Brundys. "Bring them in and we'll see what we can do," said the woman at the desk. Then she asked Mother, "But how about you? You have a fine bunch of children and you are not having it too easy?"

"Well, I hadn't really thought about it," said Mother. "We would be glad for any help we could get." No shoes in stock were wide enough for Mother's feet, but she selected shoes she thought Mary Elizabeth and I could wear.

When Mrs. Thorne came to take three of the four Brundy children to the Red Cross office to try on shoes, they had washed their feet as she asked and she brought clean pairs of socks for each. At the office the older girl and boy were given shoes of the same style as Mother had brought home for Mary Elizabeth and me. A style you couldn't help noticing, not just standard school oxfords, but two-tone brown and tan shoes with a fringed flap over the toes. Mary Elizabeth refused to wear hers and maybe they did hurt her feet. I needed shoes and reasoned that nobody I knew would see the Brundys. If they ever started to school they would be in lower grades. I worried more about being asked where I got my shoes. Though the Millers were not noted for going out of town to shop, I made up a formula I hoped would work. "I got them in Memphis." Memphis was a plausible source of Red Cross supplies and maybe I wasn't even lying.

Eventually Mother did ask Rhoda if she liked having all those men come down all the time. Rhoda hung her head and didn't say anything. Her mother-in-law (or mother) spoke up and said the men kept on coming even if they told them to stay away, "Looks like they got into the habit and can't get out of it."

Mother was not satisfied to let the question stand. She said, "Why, we can do something about that. We can get the law if we have to. You don't have to bring up your children like this."

"You've been so good to us," said old Mrs. Brundy. "Nobody been as good as you."

"Well, you keep those men away from here and I'll guarantee you enough to eat and to keep you warm."

Mother knew it was a rash promise, but she hoped that with

the help of the Lord and the Red Cross, she could make it good.

The next week, she and I walked to town together. About half way there we saw the town policeman whom I recognized as the father of a school friend. Mother said, "I am going to speak to your friend's father." I knew what about and I wanted to be as far away as possible. Mother rushed after him.

I stayed where I was, pretending I had a rock in my shoe, untying and retying it. I still couldn't help overhearing them, because Mother was excited enough to talk loud. I could hear her saying how another little baby was going to be born, and there were already four, "Now I want you to do your part. You keep those men away from there."

My friend's big father was a quiet soft-spoken man. He smiled indulgently, "Why, Mrs. Miller, you're a mighty good woman, and you've got mighty nice children. But you aren't from around here, are you? You've never seen people like these. Nothing you can do with them. Nothing's going to keep the men away from those Brundy women."

Whether the officers tried or not, whether the women tried or not, the situation remained the same. Mother and Mrs. Thorne were at the Brundy house one day when one of the men slipped out of the kitchen in his shirt and took his overalls off a nail on the door. Mother smiled when she told Mary Elizabeth and me about it. She was more embarrassed for Mrs. Thorne than for herself, "After all, I have seen a man without his pants since Mrs. Thorne has."

The friendship between the Bible ladies and the Brundys continued. While the older girl and boy could not be persuaded, even with shoes, to go to school, Mother got them started coming by our house to go to Sunday School with us. They came partly for the pancakes she gave them for breakfast and the coffee they insisted on instead of the buttermilk we drank. We hated having them go to church with us at all. I carefully put cardboard in my old shoes on Sundays, so that I didn't have to wear my Red Cross shoes like theirs. Once we were out of the house Mary Elizabeth and I stayed close together and walked far ahead of the family. The Brundys walked with Mother and Caroline and John B. who were still young enough to try to behave as Mother wanted. The first Sunday I introduced the

143

girl Arlene to my Sunday School class, hoping that they would not think that she was my friend. I left as much space as I could between us in the pew. She barely nodded her head to the teacher and neither of us spoke during class.

I was sure that, according to the Bible, Mother's idea that we should be friends of the poor was right. But I couldn't help wanting to turn away when I saw the Brundys. Why did the poor look, smell, feel so much worse to most of the people we knew in McKenzie, including Mary Elizabeth and me, than they did to Mother and Mrs. Thorne? Mrs. Thorne had tried to introduce a larger number of children from Brawnertown to her church, the U.S.A. Presbyterian, a few years before. She was finally asked not to bring them because their smell, noise, and constant need to go to the bathroom disturbed the regular members of the church. Arlene and her brother were clean and quiet and neither asked to go to the bathroom even once. But within a few weeks Mary Elizabeth and I managed to discourage them from coming by our house on Sunday mornings in spite of the pancake breakfasts, and we knew they hadn't enjoyed our company any more than we liked theirs.

The day Rhoda's baby was born, the Brundy boy knocked on our door about five in the morning, "Mammy's sick." Mother was already up praying and reading the Bible. She sent the boy back home to say that she would take care of things. Then she went to Mrs. Thorne's, who she knew would be up or wouldn't mind being waked, to start telephoning doctors. Who? Where? Plenty of doctors in the small towns in our part of the country during the Depression years, so Mother had a long list to call. One by one as the sleepy husband or wife heard who the mother and child were and where they lived, the physician refused to leave his bed. Finally Mother reached our piano teacher's husband, Dr. Follinsbee, who now spent much of the week in Nashville fitting glasses. He said that he would go by the Brundys' house and see how things were before he left McKenzie.

The baby was born all right and had his navel properly tied. Rhoda insisted that Mother name the little boy and she called him Paul, "to give him a name to live up to."

Making a baby dress was a requirement of our second-year Home Economics class. I made a little white batiste dress with embroidery for Paul. It was much easier than going to church with his older sister and brother.

At some point after Paul was born, somebody from the country brought the family a cow and Mother allowed the children to stake it in our yard for a short while because our grass was "greener." Later she saw Arlene pass several times on her way to town holding hands with a boy that Mother feared might be her half-brother or even brother. Before we moved from Spruce Street, the Brundys disappeared from the street as mysteriously as they had come.

The Follinsbees

Next to the Brundys, the people we liked least to be associated with in town were the Follinsbees. Their oddity began with the tobacco stained beard of the grandfather who could occasionally be seen on the sidewalk outside the tan brick house and its unkempt yard on a major street in town. He wasn't ashamed to tell his grandchildren that he had hidden out in the woods during the War between the States. Both Follinsbee children had slight but noticeable physical defects: the daughter, one thin arm partially paralyzed, and legs and feet that turned in so sharply that Dr. Follinsbee had a good excuse for not allowing her to wear high-heeled shoes. The boy had a walleye and a stutter and spent an endless childhood being chased and teased by other children. Dr. Follinsbee boasted that, though he was not a religious man, he had used Genesis to teach the boy to read, reinforcing the teaching by use of the strap.

Since we came to McKenzie with a little money, we may have paid for the piano which Mrs. Follinsbee offered to us when Mother signed us up with her for piano lessons, but we never paid for any lessons after the first month's. Mother must have spoken to Mrs. Follinsbee and Mrs. Follinsbee must have said something back, but it was a debt we never felt guilty about. Clearly our piano teacher cared more about having students to teach than about being paid. We fulfilled all her hopes for us when Caroline and I both won prizes in the McDowell Music Club contest that first spring.

Caroline and I were not as distressed as Mary Elizabeth by Mrs. Follinsbee's straight black hair, home-made dresses, lack of makeup, and the stomach that bulged from her otherwise stringy body. Caroline, beginning lessons, must have learned something from her. But my lessons, in the house she had rented for her piano across from the grammar school, were never very satisfactory. After a few minutes spent with *One Hundred Famous Piano Compositions,* the book Mrs. Forrest had given me in Hiseville, she spent most of any lesson hour talking about the inferiority of the other music teachers in town and all the things that had almost ruined

147

her life: her terrible stepmother, being kept out of school, her weeks with typhoid fever. An inheritance from her father helped her to go to Ward Belmont in Nashville where she studied with the European music teacher whom she called "the best in the South." The other teachers in town did not teach their students to bear down on the keys to achieve the rich tone she believed her teacher had taught her. I could not hear the difference between her playing and that of Mrs. Kelly who played at our church and wondered if she had taught me to make the sounds she talked about. I doubted that my sound was better than Mrs. Kelly's, although I enjoyed the hours I spent sight reading from old song books and even the *Famous Compositions*, especially in summer as my friends began to drop away. I hated the scantily attended recitals where Caroline and I were major stars. After several years of free lessons, Caroline and I both quit Mrs. Follinsbee. Caroline was serious enough about her music so that Mother eventually arranged to clean Mrs. Kelly's house in exchange for her more orderly and conventional lessons.

Like Mrs. Follinsbee's credentials in music, Dr. Follinsbee's medical credentials were good. "He's a smart man" neighbors would admit whenever they talked about him, but he had nearly every peculiarity one prefers not to see in a doctor. His patients expected to die ten times over before his ancient car, with windows pieced together with adhesive tape, brought him for visits to their homes. He carried a toothpick in his mouth most of the time, sometimes picked his nose, and had been known to belch when examining a patient. Almost entirely lacking in small talk, he could spend hours on opinions that required lengthy exposition: man's descent from the ape or the deleterious effect of high-heeled shoes on the female organs. If a Socialist vote was cast in McKenzie in the election of 1932, it would have been his, not because he believed in the ideas, people said, but "to be different from everybody else."

Mother and I liked the fact that he insisted that Professor Seats, the Webb High School principal, come to his front door, when it was still the custom all over the South for Negroes to go to the back. He was the only doctor Mother could get to come when Paul Brundy was born, and he did not send bills to people he knew could not pay.

The family encounter with him began with John B.'s circumcision our first year in McKenzie. In that first intimate talk with Mrs. Follinsbee about piano lessons for all of us Mother mentioned her regret that her son's birth at home in Bowling Green did not include circumcision. Mrs. Follinsbee suggested that Dr. Follinsbee could easily take care of that. Having our brother return home so painfully spraddle-legged from Dr. Follinsbee's operating room guaranteed that he would be called only as a last resort. Well after Paul Brundy's birth, and my prolonged spell of asthma and some bad nights when ephedrine did not help, Mother called him and found him in town.

Caroline and John B. hid behind the house when they heard his car in the yard after dark. Instead of the shot of adrenaline which other doctors gave me when I was the worst, he offered me calomel out of his black bag. He and Mother continued to argue for at least an hour afterward about where Christ went when he ascended from the grave. Though I was back in school two days later, maybe assisted by the natural adrenaline that came with the visit or maybe by the calomel, I hoped never to see him again.

But he was not ready to let me go. In the midst of his optical practice in Nashville a year or so later, he heard about the new allergy treatments for asthma. With Mother's consent he arranged for me to have a week's tests with an allergy specialist during Christmas vacation of my senior year in high school and offered me transportation to Nashville where he returned regularly. Mother made sure that I would not drive with him alone—he had some regular riders. She also arranged for me to stay with a friend's sister married to a well-known Cumberland Presbyterian minister.

As grateful as I should have been for the help that really changed my life, I was glad that Dr. Follinsbee was not available to give me the shots that would be required back in McKenzie after the tests. They were given to me free of charge by a high-school history teacher's doctor father whom we had not seen previously and to whom we did not owe money. With the help of all that treatment I never had another asthma attack.

Dr. Follinsbee could be rude to people in all kinds of ways and was often a bore when he felt kindly, even something of a creep. But he seemed to have decided that people did not have to like him to benefit from his knowledge and skills.

At Granddad's Bedside

I was surprised when my son Joseph asked why we had not gone back to the farm when hard times struck. Granddad had died long before Joseph was born in 1955, and he had never visited in Kentucky while the family lived on the farm. But I had talked about the good times there, and he had a vivid impression of the hard times of the Depression. Until he asked me, the question had never occurred to me. The farm was the place where we visited, not where we lived. My mother and father had agreed before they were married that they would never live on a farm. Mother may have thought of living on the farm again when Granddad got very sick in the fall of 1933.

Soon after we moved to Spruce Street, Grandmother wrote to both Anna in Akron and Mother in McKenzie about how serious matters were. Aunt Allye and Uncle Robert had their own farm to take care of and lived too far away to help regularly. Goodyear had laid off Ernest early during the Depression, and he and Anna had returned to the farm long enough for their first daughter Pat to be born, but had returned to Akron when Goodyear called Ernest back. Both sisters had reasons not to go when Grandmother wrote. Anna loved Akron and had hoped that they were now settled there. Mother was in her third year at Bethel and she would have to take four of us out of school. But both loved Granddad and both knew that Grandmother needed help. Without consulting one another, both decided to make the journey home. Somehow Daddy managed to send us the money for the trip on the Louisville and Nashville Railroad which ran from McKenzie to Bowling Green. Ernest, Anna, and Pat had already arrived from Akron, and Ernest met us at Bowling Green.

At some point on our train trip back to Kentucky Mother mentioned her concern about what would happen to the farm if Granddad died. She had not forgotten that Granddad once said that he would never have been able to pay for the farm if he hadn't had her help in the cornfield. I could not help feeling that rivalry between the two sisters had something to do with the rush to Granddad's bedside. I knew about the jealousy between Mary Elizabeth and me who were just eighteen months apart in age, but the difference in age between Mother, the oldest daughter, and Anna, the youngest child, was fourteen years, and the jealousy was even fiercer.

Granddad's success on the farm with the passing years and the more prosperous times during and after World War I made possible the indulgence of the only child left at home as well as her going away to high school in her early teens. But it was not easy for Mother to be rational about all that. She had been sure of her firstness in Granddad's heart as long as she was at home. He depended on her, a word she loved and aimed to live up to. But on her visits home after she had been away at school and work, she began to notice how companionable Granddad and her little sister had become: Anna always tagging after the big man when he went about his chores and being raised so differently from the older children. Mother and Aunt Edna and Uncle Henry had been lucky if they held a nickel in their hands from one year's end to the next; Anna had nickels and even dimes when she went to the store on Saturday afternoons. None of the other sisters had a doll buggy like Anna's. And Anna was always wearing a new dress with a little of Aunt Barbara's embroidery or smocking on it.

Except for the time in Akron, Anna remained close to home all those years that Mother was away. She went to high school in Beaver Dam and to college in Bowling Green with frequent trips home on the river boat. She brought her future husband Ernest home soon after she met him in Akron.

When we all arrived at the farm there was no question that Grandmother had first place at Granddad's bedside. She hardly left it day or night, even to eat or go to the toilet. The great bulk of him lay in his double bed in the living room, with no sound except his breathing. The doctor whom Mother and Anna had known all their lives had about given him up for dead. They decided to call in a doctor from Owensboro immediately. The new doctor gave Granddad some new medicine and held out a little more hope.

Mother and Anna divided the sitting up at night between them. There was plenty of work for everybody to do, even after Pearle Mae, a neighbor's daughter who was a former student of Anna's, came to help. Mother kept the kitchen fire going, the cream separator chunking away, and the dish and mop water flying out the back door. Anna was always carrying huge buckets of something: milk or slop for the pigs or water from the well. She let us hunt for eggs with her, and we often made the trip to the pasture for the cows at night or to take them back in the morning. We did that with Ernest, too, who carried Granddad's stick and was more likely to persuade old Hoover, the no-count shepherd-collie that replaced Towser, to come with us. The dog spent most of its time on the porch outside Granddad's bedroom.

In the way Anna raised Pat, just as in the way she taught school, we could see many of Mother's habits, plus some innovations which had come in since we were babies. Pat had her own crib in the parlor we still called Anna's Room, ate half an orange, and had cod liver oil every day. Even in this time of so much upset, Anna held Pat in her lap at least once a day while she read and sang to her. She also called her "darling" instead of "honey" and wouldn't let her say "ain't" or "nasty."

Though Granddad had called his dog "Hoover," the "4-H" name that everybody knew also stood for "hard times" and "hell," the Depression didn't seem to have changed things much at the farm. Grandmother and Granddad were as near to self-sufficient as anyone could be. They had the same good food as always, raised the animals, and bought only a few staples at what had been Uncle Henry's store. It was Granddad's illness that hung over the farm the way the Depression hung over the rest of the country.

As pathetic as he was and as dear the memory of his visiting me in Anna's Room when I had asthma during our last visit, I was still intimidated by Granddad. From the familiar conversations of other visits, at the dinner table and on the porch, and his cutting remarks when we were too much underfoot, I saw him as obsessed with the possibility that any of those close to him would make the misstep that meant they would "never get anywhere in this world." "Never getting anywhere" was to lose or never own a farm or a house, not to have money in the bank by the time you were a certain age, to go into bankruptcy or to be dependent on others. One avoided this earthly damnation by working every day, except Sundays and

Saturday afternoons, in a well-coordinated schedule of productive physical activity. Although he had talked about going to Yale or Harvard as a young man and about playing every musical instrument, I don't think he could have lived any life that involved sitting down most of the daylight hours in good weather. Teachers "worked" because they were on their feet all day. Reading a book that wasn't a school book during the daytime was laziness. Even children should be helping with the housework in any way they could or playing with the younger children to keep them out of the way of the people who had to work. People who worked were "some account," while those who didn't were "no account." The worst thing next to being a poor worker and no account was to be a "poor manager." Granddad spent most of his life paying for a farm instead of inheriting it from his father who, Civil War or no Civil War, had not been a good manager.

True, Granddad had sometimes hurt our feelings, but we were all convinced that, if he did die, he would go to heaven. He had built a world we loved. Especially during this trip, when I had a quiet minute in the Girls' Room or, as old as I was, hopping rocks down beside the barn, I turned around and thought, "Is there anywhere in the world I would rather be than here?" And each time the answer was "I would rather be here in this place we have always come back to no matter how many times we moved. I would rather be here right now than at McKenzie, in school or not in school, or in Bowling Green or Louisville or Memphis. And so would Mary Elizabeth, Caroline, and John B."

In the brilliant light of autumn, it was a beautiful world with the gentle folds and quiet colors of the hills and harvested fields. The trees along the river were still green and those in the woods were just turning. In between the river and the woods, the mowed fields were gold except for the little specks of white chickens and the occasional outcroppings of rock.

Any world my grandmother presided over was a blessed one. Her present position in the rocking chair at Granddad's side was not the usual one in which I had known her, although I had heard of those years at Aunt Evie's side and those weeks at Aunt Edna's. I knew her best moving at a quick pace to purvey food and comfort to man and beast, at the same time spreading around her an atmosphere of peaceful love. She was Mary and Martha of the Bible in the one person. And with Granddad's lifetime of ties in the community where he was so much respected as a man of property, but not too much property, and for his knowledge of men and mules, and his tree-that-can-not-be-moved integrity, we felt like princes and princesses in a privileged little kingdom. No evil could come near us, whether or not we were the king's favorite.

After the first of October, Point Pleasant Church changed its summer schedule of Sunday School and preaching in the morning to Sunday School in the afternoon and preaching once a month. While we remained at the farm for several weeks, I remember being at church only once. Our last Sunday afternoon Grandmother stayed with Granddad and Uncle Ernest drove the rest of us to church.

The after-church gathering in the darkening afternoon was much more subdued than the summer Sunday mornings I remembered from when we were younger. We got some bony hugs, one or two dry kisses from the older women, some furtive twinkles from a few of the boys and men. Mother tried to be her old enthusiastic self as she embraced one old friend or another, "Now let me tell you who this is; this woman as a little girl had the most beautiful brown hair and still does, hardly a gray hair in it." Then laughter, and the response was almost the way it was when we were younger, "Miss Mary, there never was a teacher like her."

Everybody was concerned about Granddad: "How's Mr. Elliott?"

We wandered out back when we saw that Uncle Ernest was still absorbed in conversation. On our earlier visits to the graveyard, Mother had regularly cried a little. She cried now when her eyes lit on the white obelisks of Aunt Evie's and Aunt Edna's tombstones and the broader granite of Uncle Henry's. Now she walked around the space in the family lot where Grandmother and Granddad would lie. We all remained quiet for a long time. Nobody had to be scolded about stepping on a grave or told not to climb on a tombstone. As much as Mother had struggled to acquaint us with the fact of death, the reality was still unbelievable. That anyone who had lived could ever die was as incomprehensible to me as imagining my own non-existence in the time before I was born. But observing that a man as practical as Granddad had spent money for a family lot in the cemetery for himself, and all the others to whom death would inevitably come, made it more likely. "Yes, Mary," said the old elder who had followed us out. "That's just about the lines of the Elliott lot." And we were quiet a little longer while the elder stood with his head bowed and his hands locked behind him.

I looked up and saw Uncle Ernest was coming toward us. Mother was kneeling among the autumn leaves in the unoccupied space. Her eyes were closed. Her water-slick hands with the wedding ring on her left hand were clasped together. She abruptly rose to her feet, "Well, we can go on home. He's not going to die."

"Yes," said Uncle Ernest. "We're just about the last ones here. Mrs. Elliott will be wondering where we are."

"I mean we can go back to McKenzie," said Mother. "Father isn't going to die."

Uncle Ernest took Mother's arm to guide her back to the car. The rest of us, including Anna holding Pat's hand, straggled behind. Knowing Mother was a little shaky, Uncle Ernest urged her to sit in the front seat of the car.

Back at the farm we tiptoed in. Grandmother, pushing her combs in her hair on each side and clicking her false teeth, gave a little start. She had obviously been sleeping in her chair. "Charley's much better."

It seemed wonderful to all of us that Mother's and Grandmother's words came so close together. It wasn't the only time that Mother had some sudden revelation that seemed almost supernatural. But it spoke of some change in her as well as Granddad. We were free to go back to McKenzie. If she had ever thought of remaining at the farm, that was behind her now. We children needed to be in school. She had the year of classes and her dissertation to complete.

Anna and Ernest stayed on at the farm after we left that fall and eventually bought it at a price Mother considered a giveaway. When Pat was ready for high school, they all moved to Beaver Dam, Grandmother and Granddad, too, in a little house of their own. Ernest worked the farm from Beaver Dam and nobody lived in the farm house for a few years. Granddad died in 1944. When the farmhouse burned in the early '50s, we all mourned. "Faulty wiring," we were told. The fire took with it so much we remembered.

Dates and Dancing

"How did you get along when you were a teenager?" a granddaughter not far from being a teenager herself once asked me.

John B. began giving the girl he liked quarter boxes of chocolate-covered cherries at Christmas when he was in the third grade. A young preacher at Bethel College fell in love with Caroline when she was fourteen, and she was married when she was sixteen. When Mary Elizabeth was a junior in high school, one of her many boyfriends gave her a wrist watch, almost as significant a pledge of affection as an engagement ring.

Not with the same boys and certainly with no thought of early marriage, during my high school years I would have liked a relationship, similar to some of theirs, with a member of the opposite sex. But with the setbacks of my asthma and the breakup of the friendship with Lloyd and the friends in seventh grade, I never found my place among either boys or girls during the high school years. My hair remained straight, slicked back behind my ears. I did not even begin wearing pinky orange Tangee lipstick until I was a junior. I was notoriously bookish.

Harris Collier was the boy who loaned me a pencil when Lloyd gave me paper on the first day of seventh grade. I saw him sometimes during the year with the Signal-Hide-and-Seek crowd. His family and Lloyd's were old friends and together their mothers had pushed them in their baby carriages before they could walk. After the Temperance Essay contest we passed each other on the sidewalk one day, beside his family's yellow brick house on the corner of Stonewall and Magnolia, and he spoke to me, "I am glad you beat that old Lloyd Allison." A year later, the summer after eighth grade, I remembered those words. Right there lying on the grass under the apple tree on Laurel Street, I decided to be in love with him.

Boys were then added to the miseries of my relations with girls. There was an iron bar and padlock between students who dated and those who didn't date. "You don't date do you?" asked a friend new in town who did date. Speaking of some friend of a boyfriend of hers who asked about me, she said, "I told him you didn't date." I wanted to say, "No, but I'd like to," but the words never came. You could see the homeliest, raggediest girls downtown on Saturday night and they all had dates. With Roosevelt's new Civilian Conservation Corps ("C.C.C.") a couple of miles from town, any girl could get a date if her parents permitted it. I never met any of the C.C.C. crowd and did not particularly want to. A friend that I had liked to talk with about books from the library was dropped by everyone when her stomach began to swell after some contact with one of them and she quit school sophomore year. But I did not like the fact that boys, and girls too, just looked at me and decided I wasn't grown-up enough to date.

I often thought it would have made a difference if Mother had approved of dancing, or even tolerated it, although I later knew some girls who felt the same way about drinking. Only their scruples against imbibing alcoholic beverages kept them from a brilliant social life.

While some people in McKenzie considered the town Old South, it had not gone in for balls in the past and dancing was new. The Puritans had far outnumbered the Cavaliers in town, and for most of McKenzie's existence, drinking, card-playing, and dancing had been the most popular of other people's sins for rousing sermons. Of the deadly three, dancing had the most to offer the imagination of the fire-and-brimstone preachers: "And here's this man with his belly plastered against the silk-sheathed abdomen of this woman."

Few drank among the high school crowd in those first years after Prohibition was repealed. We had all taken "the Pledge" in grade school, never to touch alcohol in any form, and had renewed it annually. I could not imagine drinking, as long as I remained at home, any more than I could imagine committing adultery or murder. Most of the young people I knew had the same attitude as I.

But as for dancing, suddenly the bars against it were let down, and everybody in my old Signal-Hide-and-Seek crowd was dancing. Just how it got started was never clear. Neighbors on Spruce Street were suspicious that the young society women who had made bridge playing the thing to do among their friends had a hand in it. As the stories circulated of those eighth-grade parties where kissing games were played, a few parents may have decided that some "planned activities" were necessary. At any rate when the young people made up their minds that they wanted to learn to dance, there was Lloyd's old dance teacher to help them along, and most of her older students quit tap, ballet, and toe, and went on to ballroom. By the time she left town to go up North for more graduate work, everybody in that generation who wanted to learn to dance and was going to had learned.

Dancing or not dancing also put you on one side or the other of a gulf just as dating and not dating did, and whether you danced depended partly on whether you went to parties where there was dancing. Mother's rule, in general, was to let us do what we wanted if she saw no harm in it. If I had ever actually been invited to a dance, her rule would have had one of its hardest tests. As a girl Mother could "play-party" all night. This recreation of Saturday nights at the country school houses in Kentucky used much the same steps as square dancing—with singing, clapping hands, and sometimes a fiddle supplying music. But she had seen and heard enough of ballroom dancing during her term at the University of Kentucky to decide that it "arouses the passions." Since I was never asked to a dancing party, I proudly said to whoever was interested: "My family doesn't believe in dancing." When a new girl entered my high school one of the first questions asked was "Do you dance?" "Oh, you don't?" became enough of a bond to invite her to join the group who had lunch together around one of the big pot-bellied stoves at old McTyeire school, the former Methodist private school to which the public high school had moved to make way for the grammar school when the old school burned down.

Aside from dancing, the crowning of the football queen and the football banquet were the activities where the not "in" students were the most "out." With our season tickets Mary Elizabeth and I attended all the high school football games. The bleachers along our side of the field were occupied only by a few mothers and grandfathers. Most of the high school fans ran groaning, cheering, singing up and down the field with the players. We knew the life history and every manifestation of the personality of each boy on our team, but the members of the opposing teams from nearby small towns were facelessly identifiable only by their colors. It was exhilarating to be so sure of who you were for and who you were against. I kept my eyes on Harris Collier, his beautifully turned wrists stretching well beyond the sleeves of his jersey and his taut muscles and mobile Adam's apple signaling his nerviness.

Before the last game of the season, a football queen, elected by the students at a nickel a vote, was crowned by the football captain after she and the court she had chosen marched down the field. The girls in the court wore their prettiest fall dresses and big yellow chrysanthemums. Along with the players' dates not in the court, all of them would attend the football banquet in the high school home economics room housed in a former McTyeire dormitory.

Year after year, as the days before and after the crowning of the queen came and went, I yearned to play some larger role than I had before. Lloyd Allison was elected queen our sophomore year. There were other girls in those lunch meetings around the stove who spoke more openly of their hopes and disappointments, their hatred of the boys who had not asked them to the banquet, and their low opinion of the looks and intelligence of the girls who had been asked. I wonder what Mother, who so much wanted us to have whatever we wanted, would have done if she had known how Mary Elizabeth and I felt. Would she have tried to joke us out of it? "Oh, you don't care about those little fellows." Or would she have stepped up to Coach Glass or Coach Burkhalter or some likely parents to ask for a couple of handy players for her girls? That was her way: either make up your mind you don't want what you thought you had your heart set on or go out and get it.

In spite of no dates, I had some moments of keen pleasure with boys. Some were whenever Jim Williams, the son of the popular doctor, came along in his brilliantly painted green and white Model T Ford and invited me, along with everyone else he passed, to jump on. The happiest possible beginning of a school day was to be asked to hop onto the running board of the Model T and go bouncing along with the wind blowing through my hair, and the old Signal-Hide-and-Seek crowd hanging on all around and hugging one another to keep from falling off.

I was delighted by any occasion when I could watch Harris,

actually every day in school, but also at Covington's Drug Store where he worked behind the soda fountain, and at football games, class parties, picnics, the Senior play. Although Lloyd Allison could be seen with a number of different boys, she was often with Harris. I watched him kneel to help her with her galoshes on the snowy night of a class party.

At school I looked for chances to catch Harris's eye. I eventually learned that half the girls in the class did the same, and he bestowed the largess of his intense brown-eyed glances on all. I always jumped when he spoke to me to request an eraser or to ask me to read a word on the blackboard. The agitation tickled him and the row of students around him and may have given away my infatuation.

By the time I had firmly fixed on Harris as my secret love, I no longer had a best girl friend and I never mentioned my attachment to anyone. Now that I think of it, neither did the rest of "half the girls in the class." In McKenzie High School unrequited love was a subject for nothing except wild ridicule. The attitude of my classmates was much the same as Mother's on other subjects: you succeeded in winning the object of your interest, transferred the interest to someone or something attainable, or kept quiet about it. With my reputation for studiousness, not dancing, not wearing makeup and not dating, I had no hope of enticing any boyfriend, so I kept quiet.

Miss Edna

I had no idea when I first met Miss Edna Stephenson that she would take the place of the girlfriends and boyfriends that I did not have in high school. Even before she spoke to me, I had noticed the tall thin woman with a dip of chin very nearly parallel to her long nose at the McKenzie Public Library, a maze of bookshelves on the balcony above Cannon's Drug Store. She wore a calico house dress a few inches above the ankle and some strange arrangement of net, ribbon, and artificial flowers over her chopped-off straight gray hair. If I had seen anyone to ask about her, I would have said, "Who is that funny looking old woman?" The deferent attention paid to her by Lloyd Allison's mother and the other society ladies who were acting as librarians, however, indicated that if you couldn't mention Miss Edna without making fun of her, you had better not speak of her at all. Her own manners, as she thanked the women for a book held on reserve, had the assurance her hat and dress lacked.

Maybe months later, Mrs. Thorne invited me to drive with her to visit some friends who turned out to be Miss Edna and her shut-in mother. She asked me to bring some of my music books because they had a piano and liked to hear young people play.

Strangely, in that small town I had never noticed Miss Edna's house any more than I had noticed Miss Edna. I picked houses to pay attention to that I would have liked to live in, and I would never have chosen that weather-beaten gabled structure, separated from the street leading out of town by a low iron fence and gate and almost hidden by two house-high fir trees.

Mrs. Thorne and I climbed the steep steps onto the narrow, downward leaning porch which almost threw you into the street again. In a town where few people locked their doors, Miss Edna had to unlatch the screen door, but standing back to hold it open for us she did not seem so grotesque at home as she had at first glance in the library. Not wearing that hat helped, and so did the glad look on her sharp-featured face. Mrs. Thorne who went around in a froth of chiffon scarves and nice-smelling toilet water made everyone feel brighter as she called them "darling" and blessed their hearts.

Miss Edna invited us from the hall into the cool gloom of the living room where the shades were drawn. Although the temperature outside was warm, a little fire was burning on the hearth. "Mother felt chilly," she explained. To the right of the living room door, Mrs. Stephenson was propped nearly upright against her crochet-edged starched pillow cases in the bed with high headboards like those in my grandparents' house. Her white nightgown trimmed with tatting and white embroidery was beautiful, and her white hair was perfectly in place. Both comfortable and alert, she looked as though she planned to be there for a long time.

Miss Edna made room for Mrs. Thorne to sit between her mother's bed and the square old-fashioned piano with its spindle stool centered at middle C. She then deftly maneuvered me the length of the room toward the pair of cane-bottom chairs by a window. The awkward woman at the library disappeared; so did the equally awkward teenager. Miss Edna saw before her only the bookish girl Mrs. Thorne had promised to bring, good at Latin and obliging at the piano, with straight hair, like her own, bobby-pinned above the ears, and with no makeup. She talked fast.

"Of course I went to old McTyeire academy. I loved Latin and I studied Greek one year with Mr. Jamie Robins who went on to teach at Vanderbilt after McTyeire closed. Father thought that I should stay at home for one year after I graduated. But I was all prepared to go to Vanderbilt the following fall. Then Father became ill, dreadfully ill, Mother was frail and I stayed at home to nurse him."

The picture was startlingly vivid to me, especially with the whiff of Vicks Salve in the air and the faint smell of urine from the china pot under her mother's bed. A mere breath had blown her from the grand June day when she stood as a girl graduate on the platform at McTyeire to this moment in this room. Without ever having realized her dream of going to Vanderbilt, she was now a maiden lady considerably older than my mother. The texts of her last year at school occupied a shelf easier to get at than her father's library behind glass doors. Even her geometry book was there because she wanted not to forget anything she had ever learned. The classics, however, were her real love. Her Greek had improved since academy days, and she could read Latin more fluently than Mother who had not read it for some years.

At a pause in our animated conversation, Mrs. Thorne suggested that I come to the piano and play something for the ladies. Miss Edna gently picked up the green book of *One Hundred Famous Piano Compositions* which I had laid on the piano when I came in and looked reverently at the postage-stamp sized pictures of the musicians arranged on the cover like high school graduates on the cover of a yearbook. She was thrilled by the very names of the musicians: "Do you play anything by Brahms?" she asked hesitantly, "Or Mozart? Mozart is one of Mother's favorite composers."

Mrs. Thorne rushed the compliments and apologies a little as we were leaving, but both Miss Edna and her mother had a chance to speak of how nice my touch was and how out of tune the piano, but what a good tone it had anyway.

I meant to visit the two women again soon, but it was awkward. The mother who had seemed so well the day of our visit got pneumonia, and within a month the *McKenzie Banner* carried the news of her death. I had never known what to say to people when their relatives died. I envied my grandmother and the nicest of my aunts and cousins back in Kentucky who simply threw their arms around the bereaved and cried. Finally when Mrs. Thorne reminded me that I ought to go to see Miss Edna, I nodded my head, picked up my book of *Famous Piano Compositions* a few days later, and ambled along the half mile of graveled road and broken sidewalk between our house and Miss Edna's. When I knocked on the front door and failed to hear her step immediately, I half hoped that she wasn't at home. I was relieved when I heard her struggling with the lock; at last I was doing what I knew I ought to. She was as cordial as if I had been coming every week, as she drew me into the living room and began telling me how her mother had enjoyed my music.

That afternoon of my first visit alone, she proposed that we begin reading Virgil's *Aeneid* which was not taught in my high school and might be useful when I applied to college. I had recently won a silver loving cup in a West Tennessee second-year Latin contest and agreed. She loaned me the text she had studied at McTyeire, a small black book, crumbling to brown at the edges, with tiny print, and suggested that I start with the first line, *"Armo virumque cano...."*

Our meetings settled into a pattern. First, the formal lesson when I translated however many lines I had been assigned in as fluent and natural a reading voice as I could command. She then read the Latin aloud to me sounding out the dactylic hexameters. Each visit I took my *Famous Piano Compositions* and played three or four selections. For refreshments she set out at a little table Cambric tea—hot water with milk and sugar—which I had read about in English children's books, but never tasted before. Now and then she gave me a cookie or a bit of cake a neighbor had brought in. Toward the end of the summer, she gave me the first ripe figs I ever ate, planted by her father against the sunny side of the house in the grassy backyard.

When school began in the fall, even if I couldn't keep up the pretense of reading Virgil, I was in the habit of seeing Miss Edna once or twice a week, and she counted on my visits more and more. She was usually eager to read aloud any letters she had received since my last visit, letters from more friends of the past than I would have expected. I was surprised to hear that she had run a photographer's shop for several years between the time of her father's death and her mother's becoming an invalid.

She pulled down boxes of old photographs to show me what the friends who wrote the letters had looked like when they were younger. The contrast between the photographic details of the surroundings and the look of the faces was startling. Every curl of the old wicker chairs, every tuck and ruffle of the dresses, and the puffs and curls of the old-fashioned hair styles were clear; so were the features of the faces, but there was also a certain glory about them, as if Miss Edna had dreamed them instead of photographed them. The glances of brides, soldiers, and buttoned-up grandmothers fell directly on the viewer. All had their own beauty, conveying to the world something of what they were that could hardly be read any other way. I could see why the friends she had made from that era had remained friends, and that her life had indeed been richer than I had at first allowed.

"Why did you give up photography?" I asked her one day.

"Well, there was the illness in the family," she said, "and

there were all those babies."

"You mean the babies misbehaved and were a nuisance?"

"No, there were so many and they were so dull. Oh, I liked babies well enough, and Mother loved them. But can you imagine days and weeks of nothing but photographing babies? At first Mother helped me with them, but when she wasn't well enough to take them off my hands, I simply had to give up the business."

I was almost as shocked as I had been when a northern professor's wife told me that she didn't like *Hamlet.* In the world I had known babies were as immune to discriminating criticism as the classics.

We also read aloud the poetry from my school books. And we talked a great deal about writers and their lives. Miss Edna wanted all artists to be exemplary in their sexual lives and at least minimally orthodox in their religion. Sometimes her regard for a writer's work blurred or softened her judgment of his morals. Shelley, the author of "Ode to a Skylark," an atheist? Wordsworth had an illegitimate child? She simply denied both charges. That George Eliot had lived with a man out of wedlock seemed to be pretty well established and Miss Edna admired her novels the less for it, although she loved, "Oh may I join the choir invisible/ Of those immortal dead who live again...."

When I discovered Walt Whitman whom she did not care for at all, I got the impression that she believed godliness, sexual probity, and rhyme went together. She also encouraged me to read aloud any writing of my own required in school or for the school paper. She always gave me full attention, did not praise perfunctorily, but showed by a cocked head or brightness of eye what pleased her, and made not too unrealistic suggestions for improvement where it was needed.

More and more of our quarrels were about modern literature or modern novels. While Miss Edna seldom quoted the Bible as Mother and Mrs. Thorne did, she found Philippians 4:8 indispensable: *Finally, brethren, whatsoever things are true, whatsoever things are honest, whatsoever things are just, whatsoever things are pure, whatsoever things are lovely, whatsoever things are of good report.... think on these things.*

I was strongly conscious of not wanting to think only of things that were considered *honest* and *pure* and *of good report* in McKenzie. I wanted to know about Catholicism and agnosticism and adultery, about George Bernard Shaw and Oscar Wilde, labor problems, and socialism. All the kissing and fooling around with stocking tops that my classmates were experiencing in the back seats of cars, I was getting from books now, but I didn't want to live in books and daydreams forever.

We gave each other some of the same kinds of pain and pleasure, uncertainty and suspense that I was familiar with in other friendships. I liked Miss Edna's praise and when I didn't receive it I liked her less. She wanted me to be impressed, and to agree with her, and when I didn't she was cool and disturbed. After a particularly heated discussion I was likely to leave as though nothing had happened and then stay away a week or more. I returned the same way, without apology, taking up some dropped thread of conversation, very conscious of my friend's relief at my return.

We never embraced except when I was leaving town for one reason or another. I was aware of her touch primarily when I felt a bony arm thrust through mine as we walked halfway down the block toward home on summer evenings. I heard often how much my companionship meant to her: "My life has been lonely."

Miss Edna talked about being lonely nearly every time I saw her. But unlike some other people who described themselves as lonely, she was choosy about the company she kept. Unless it was someone aesthetically or intellectually pleasing to her, the company didn't count. Good friends were mostly distant or dead. She refused to replace those loves with comfortable everyday comings and goings. As for me, my need was as great as hers for someone to share my experiences and some thoughts and even to quarrel with about serious matters. On several occasions either by putting me in touch with old friends who would be useful to me, or by giving me money out of the carefully reckoned income that allowed for milk and sugar but no tea, Miss Edna offered me a foothold up the rock of the world.

The one person I never talked to her about was Daddy, especially after he went away.

My Religion—Joining the Church

I was very young when I began to dream of God's pleasure in making the world. His delight in inventing and creating bluebirds, chickadees, woodpeckers and even sparrows. The enormous variety of flowers and every baby born. Characters in both the Old and New Testaments were almost as alive to me as anyone I knew.

Still I did not join the church until I was almost as old as Mother when she professed religion. Back on North Stonewall Street I had surprised myself and shocked Mother and my sister when I threw a hot sweet potato and hit Mary Elizabeth on the cheek. I cannot remember the exact provocation, just the feeling that I had had enough. She was too stunned to do anything except grab her cheek and burst into tears. Tears were rare for her, it was usually she who made other people cry. Mother counted on me to be the "good girl" and was troubled enough to discuss the incident with an older professor at the college. She told me that he had urged her "to get me into the church as soon as possible." I was a little ashamed that I was not ashamed—throwing that sweet potato had actually felt good and I resented Mother's bringing the professor into it.

But that was a rare disagreement. Once the Signal-Hide-and-Seek and Lloyd Allison crowd became the "dancing crowd," and I felt sorry for myself for not having a best friend, it came to me, "Why, of course, I have Mother." There were the after-school talks and the long nights we spent together when I had asthma. I did not tell her about my secret high-school love, and she did not risk scaring me with her worst fears and anxieties about Daddy's lack of a job. But we probably talked to each other more than either of us talked to anyone else and often about religion.

As I got older, I heard little in Sunday School or in the pulpit that fit in with my ideas about God. I suggested in a Sunday School discussion one Christmas that in their poverty Christ's parents, Joseph and Mary, might be "like sharecroppers." The teacher winced and said, "Oh no, not like sharecroppers." It was important to me that Mother thought I was more nearly right than the teacher.

"Blessed are the meek: for they shall inherit the earth."

Out of the whole range of Scripture I was exposed to, I was most interested in the *Book of Job*, which Mother sometimes read to me when I was sick, and the Sermon on the Mount as it is written in Matthew 5, 6, and 7. The fact that much of the Sermon was hard made it likely to be right. I may have thought about those chapters more outside of church than in, and many of my thoughts were not charitable. When I thought about how few friends I had at school or our hard times at home, I translated the chapters so as to make them as favorable as possible to the Millers and as damaging as possible to "other people." "The meek," "the merciful," "the pure in heart," "They which are persecuted for righteousness' sake"—some of those words applied to each of us. But some of our neighbors were surely laying up for themselves treasures on earth and arraying themselves at much more thought and expense than the lilies of the field. Mrs. Thorne, the radical giver, was the only person I knew who gave her cloak as well as her coat. Much of my serious thought time was spent berating others and ourselves for not being more like her.

Meanwhile, if anyone had asked me about Matthew 7:1, "Judge not that ye be not judged," I would have said, "I'm not judging anyone, I just see how things are." What about "Love your enemies, bless them that curse you, do good to them that hate you?" Well, people didn't exactly hate us; most of them were just rather indifferent, or so it often seemed. Was it quibbling to say that you could be indifferent to those who were indifferent to you? Yes, it was quibbling, if you really hated them, and I sometimes thought I did, people like the doctor who stopped his car and yelled out the window at me when I was on the way to school: "Tell your mammy that she owes me three dollars."

Though preachers in a college town did not bring "Hell" into their sermons every Sunday, it lurked in the question of whether you were "saved." At the revival meetings which we attended regularly several times a year, at our church and others, "Hell" was openly shouted about as arms waved. Mother having told us when we were little that only God knew who would go to hell, I allowed myself to forget about it with respect to myself and anyone I loved.

For years I allowed myself to believe that our baptism as

infants had "saved" us. Infant baptism was uncommon in the small towns we lived in both in Kentucky and Tennessee, and I became more uneasy as I observed that almost no parents, no matter how caring and intelligent, had taken advantage of that opportunity to help assure their children's salvation. In McKenzie we continued to attend some of the services of revival meetings at any of the major churches as we always had in the towns we lived in. More and more of the young people my age went down the aisle to the altar when the invitation to join the church was given. I had not been present when Lloyd Allison and Rowena Everett went together at a meeting at the Methodist Church the year we were in seventh grade, but heard about it later.

Ministers in town and in the country had many different formulae for issuing the invitation : "Don't you want to come to Jesus?" "Come to the Lord?" "Give your heart to Jesus?" "Be saved?" I felt that my answer to all these questions had been "yes" for as long as I could remember. But there was also, "Do you recognize that you are a miserable sinner?" While I knew that I was not as good as Mother and Mrs. Thorne sometimes seemed to think (I was very careful to keep them thinking it), I was certain that I was not that bad! From the time that I almost followed Ila Mae across the other pew-sitters' knees to the aisle at my grandparents' Point Pleasant Church, I knew that I would eventually make the journey. Meanwhile I feared that I was yearly becoming more vulnerable to the conscientious people, like Granddad's aunt, who took him by the elbow and led him to the altar. Only the fact that most people assumed that Mother's oldest daughter, pious me, had gone earlier spared me.

Finally, soon after my fifteenth birthday, I planned with Mary Elizabeth, Caroline, and John B. that, rather than waiting for a revival, one ordinary Sunday when the usual invitation was given we would all join the church together. I hardly heard any of the service that day because I was so anxious; the minister might inadvertently omit the call to the altar as he sometimes did, or he might put it in terms that would be embarrassing: "If you feel yourself to be a miserable sinner...." Mary Elizabeth or I might be, but I was sure that Caroline was not; John B. was too young to be much of a sinner. It worked out much as I had hoped. The minister asked anyone who would like to join the church to come forward while the congregation sang the last hymn. I gave the signal on the last verse of "Just as I Am": "You all coming?"

At home after church, John B. said, "I wish I'd joined the Methodist Church instead." He wasn't too young to know that many of the people we wanted most to be like, people such as Allison and Rowena, went to the Methodist Church rather than the Cumberland Presbyterian.

When I try to think whom I had in mind among our neighbors in McKenzie who could not be considered among the blessed of the Sermon on the Mount, I sometimes find it hard to remember. I suppose, first of all: snooty high school kids who did not like me and didn't ask me to their parties, the doctors who wouldn't come when Paul Brundy was born, or store owners who wouldn't give us credit when they should have known we hated to ask and wouldn't have asked if our need had not been embarrassingly pressing. But many of the citizens of McKenzie were people Daddy would have called "mighty nice," if he had known them. More people than Mrs. Thorne, Aunt Grace, and Miss Edna Stephenson were kind to us. Even before she met her special friend at the Sewing Room, Mother said that she never saw the time when she couldn't go to one neighbor or another and borrow some small essential amount of money from five cents to a few dollars. A woman whose husband was an officer out at the C.C.C. camp joined Mrs. Thorne's Bible class; for as long as they were in town she gave Mother $10 a month for clothes as a part of her program of tithing.

Borrowing was one of the mechanisms by which the whole town lived. Although I didn't dance when I was in high school, I wore an evening dress on several different occasions, always for Mrs. Follinsbee's hateful recitals. I borrowed a dress from one high school friend or another, sometimes from someone whom I barely knew. If company were coming, you could borrow anything from a table and chairs to a tablecloth, dishes, knives, and forks. Or if they were spending the night, as Mrs. Hardwick, Mother's friend, sometimes did when she was recruiting students for the Bowling Green College of Business, you could borrow a cot and sheets and blankets. If you were going away, you could borrow luggage or a hat or shoes.

You could borrow a recipe, several of the ingredients necessary to make it, and the utensil to cook it in. Or, if you were sewing, you could borrow a pattern, scissors, pins, and needles, and if your sewing machine broke down, you could go to a neighbor's—that would have been Aunt Grace—and stitch up your garment on her machine. Rakes, hoes, shovels, lawn mowers passed up and down the street.

Lunches and snacks neighbors brought me when I was sick in bed were common forms of kindness. The sickbed trays of Mrs. Meador on N. Stonewall were exquisite with all kinds of soups, breads, and sandwich fillings that I had never tasted before. Along with the food, she sometimes put a columbine or delphinium on the tray. Aunt Sis, next door to us on Spruce Street, was a white-haired little woman with hanging cheeks. Every day or so when I was sick, she would come pushing in the front door with whatever was left from her husband's lunch and sit down twinkling and trying to make small talk until I had managed to get down every bite of the soggy peach pie or burned potato soup.

Another visitor I had when I was sick on Spruce Street was the grandmother of little Paul, old Mrs. Brundy who was supposed to have started the women in her family wrong. If she knew I was at home, she was likely to stop to warm herself at the living room fire before she went on to town. "Tell the boys to keep they hands to theyselves," she warned me as she left.

All the people whom I remember as being kind were careful to guard our feelings: "Pay when you can," "It's a tithe," "Keep it as long as you need it."

On Relief

As 1933 became 1934 and 1934 became 1935, things did not get any easier. Those were the years we lived on Spruce Street, with Mrs. Thorne facing Magnolia at one end of the street and the Brundy family in their shanty at the other. Mother was more and more strained.

One weekend in the fall of 1935 when Daddy was at home he and Mother kept on talking in front of the fire in the living room after she had blown out the light in the lamp and we children were in bed. Caroline and I slept in the big double bed on the other side of the room from the fireplace. Caroline was already asleep. With my arms under my head, I could see Daddy sitting on one of the straight kitchen chairs, his elbows on his knees and his face between his hands. Mother sat in a straight chair rather than her usual rocker, so that she could be closer to him. They had been talking for some time when I heard Daddy say, "I drove fast tonight." Mother put her arm around his shoulder, "I'm glad you wanted to see us, darling." Daddy said, "I drove fast because I wanted to die. If I had driven over an embankment and killed myself, our kids would be better off. How is it possible for a man to have a wife like you and a bunch of fine children like ours and not be able to make a living?"

Mother drew closer to him. "Now that the children are older, it can't be as bad as that time in Texas when Mary Elizabeth and U.T. were babies. You got sick before you could collect for the maps you had sold."

"That was bad, darling, but there has never been anything like this thing they call 'the Depression.' People everywhere just like us. I had hoped it would be over by now but it is worse than ever. Nobody's got any money. Can't chip anything loose anywhere."

"What about Mr. Roosevelt?" Mother said. "People keep saying that he is going to help and there is a program or two around town."

Daddy said, "I would rather die than break rocks like a convict. That's what those fellows on WPA have to do." (WPA was the

Works Progress Administration, the New Deal agency offering jobs at that time.)

They went to bed in the back room where they slept when Daddy was at home and left the door open a crack. I could hear the swoosh of their dropped clothes and the creak of the bedsprings as they got into bed. Daddy was crying—maybe the first time I ever heard him cry. Then they were talking again. Mother said, "I would rather do anything than have nothing to go on. Maybe I could get on the WPA. There's a sewing program for women." I think that was the night Daddy promised that he would not take his life.

Not long after that weekend, one of the women in Mrs. Thorne's Bible class told Mother that her "nigger" had left her, and she would just as soon pay Mother to clean her house as the "nigger." She was an old woman from the country who had come into some money when a rich relative died. Mother said that she was good-hearted if ignorant, and began going over to wash the woman's bathrooms and scrub her kitchen floor. Her pay turned out to be left over biscuits and buttermilk and she was asked to use the toilet in the basement. Following her policy of never keeping anything from us, she told Mary Elizabeth and me about the situation. We were outraged and refused to eat any of the biscuits or to drink the buttermilk. For a few days Mother hardly ate anything else and she went on working for the woman. She claimed the poor old thing needed help as much as anybody. We suspected that she was tolerant of the woman because she liked talking about religion as much as Mother. After a few days Mother reported that she had had it out with her employer and would receive $3 a week for her work.

Unbeknownst to me but apparently known to Mary Elizabeth, Mother went to town one day when she was not working for the woman and inquired about the WPA sewing program for women.

There is some disagreement in the family about whether she began work on the program before or after Daddy left home. A trustworthy friend in the government told our brother John, when he was a little more grown-up, that our father had gone away so that Mother could take the WPA job, the government rule being that women could not work on WPA if their husbands were at home. Whatever the government policy was, and in the beginning it seemed to change almost from day to day, Mother was all signed up to work when Daddy left.

The signing up was a memorable occasion. Mary Elizabeth had entered high school that fall and occasionally we made the long walk home from old McTyeire together. We had turned into Spruce Street and passed Mrs. Thorne's garden when we were close enough to home to see a car with a government seal on the door parked in our yard. "There's that man," Mary Elizabeth said and pointed.

"What man?" I asked.

"The one who is going to put us 'On Relief.'" She made it sound as though somebody was going to lock us up in the city jail with the open toilets and the drunks. My sister Caroline points out that we were never really "On Relief"; WPA people had to work and Mother always worked, but feeling disgraced, as we did, we always called it "On Relief."

Inside the house was a sandy-haired young man in his twenties who had come around to investigate us. Mother had offered him the cane-bottomed chair that sagged the least and he was sitting by the fire, writing her answers to his questions on a form. Caroline and John B. were sitting in other chairs taking it all in, and Mother introduced Mary Elizabeth and me. We backed right out of the living room into the kitchen as though the whole procedure had nothing to do with us. Mother had already started a fire in the kitchen stove for supper and Mary Elizabeth started making corn bread. I sat down at the kitchen table to continue reading *Anna Karenina*. It was exciting to find it in the school library's *Harvard Classics* after I learned about it in a list of the "world's ten greatest novels" in the *Harper's Magazine* Mrs. Thorne had given me. Mother soon called Mary Elizabeth and me back into the living room and insisted that all of us do something to show how talented we were. In contrast to Mary Elizabeth who saw it as a punishment, Mother behaved as though the small sums the government would pay her for work in the WPA Sewing Room were a reward for unusual performance. Caroline and I both played the piano. John B. showed the man his big ball of tin foil. Mary Elizabeth gave him a piece of the corn bread she had just made.

Whether Mother began in the fall or after Daddy left in January—the red tape might have taken that long—she was permitted to work in the town Sewing Room, making clothes for people who must have been poorer than we were because we were never offered any of those clothes. There was the usual struggle with our pride. As much as we hated for anybody to know that Mother expected to be a preacher, we hated even more for it to be known that she worked with the women employed at that Sewing Room. No one I knew in high school had a mother who worked there. No matter how reduced their circumstances, other mothers whose children were lucky enough to make it to high school did not work for the WPA. Mother claimed she did not mind. Any money was better than no money. And she was interested in the women she met and made good friends with a few of them.

One woman came from people of a good background, as good as ours, if not better. The woman's mother, a member of one of the old families in town, had gone to Ward Belmont in Nashville, and she to McTyeire, the Methodist private school, where Miss Edna and a few students from "nice families" in McKenzie went before it closed. Her husband was disabled and she needed the sewing job. She was important to Mother, both as a friend and because she was able to save a little money between paychecks and could loan the $2 or $3 that Mother nearly always needed before pay day. They came to really love one another.

Mother did not hold herself separate from the other women that were not as well educated nor as refined in speech and manners as this friend. She found out what a hard time many of them had with husbands who drank and boys in jail. She learned plenty of gossip about the elite of the town, too. Many of the nice houses sheltered some scandal or tragedy which we hadn't heard about because we hadn't lived in McKenzie long enough, or Mother had not taken time to sit down and listen to gossip as she had the opportunity to do now. Forced to sit at her machine with all those informed tongues running on, she heard about the weak hearts and the cancer, as well as the houses sold or about to be for their mortgages or taxes, the colored children fathered by prominent white men, and the men taken in for sodomy or child molesting. She never reported to us day by day on the hardship and the scandal. But over the years, she would mention this or that. When we asked her how she knew, she always said, "Why, I guess I learned that down at the Sewing Room."

One of the things she never got used to was the women's smoking. She speculated that they tried to show their respect for her by putting out their cigarettes when she came in or by smoking in the toilet.

The Last Trip Home

During the terrible fall of 1935 when he was hardly sending home any money at all, Daddy was not idle. In fact he made the contacts that allowed him to try to sell two different new products.

After the despairing weekend when he had promised Mother that he would not kill himself, he seemed to acquire new energy and he came home the next time with a large picture book, the kind we now call a "coffee-table book," about World War I. He told us that he was going to sell it to every high school in Kentucky and Tennessee. If principals and superintendents thought they could not afford it, he would approach local chapters of the American Legion and the Veterans of Foreign Wars about making a gift of it to the local high school.

His being a soldier in World War I was almost as important to him as being a Texan. If Mother's theme song was "What a Friend We Have in Jesus," he whistled and sometimes sang "It's a Long, Long Way to Tipperary" and "Pack up Your Troubles in Your Old Kit Bag." Though he had not gone overseas he had risked his life for his country in that hospital in San Antonio where so many soldiers died of flu. His army uniform with the cavalry hat and wrap-around leggings (what he was wearing when he walked into Mother's school in 1919) went with us through all the moves we made before McKenzie.

If believing in a product would enable him to sell it, this book should have been the perfect commodity. He knew the names of all the war's battles, the generals and the outstanding soldiers, including the Tennessean, Sergeant York. Mother, too, remembered the war days as thrilling and her enthusiasm for the book was genuine. I, however, was under the spell of one of those brilliant young teachers the school board was smart enough to hire in hard times. "Mr. Bill" (my secret name for him in a time when men teachers were called by their last name and women still by their first) taught my classes in Ancient History and English II. Somewhere between Thucydides and *Macbeth*, he pressed his concern about issues of peace and war in the world of the early thirties. He told us about young people in England who had taken "the Oxford oath," swearing they would never go to war again, and read us an anti-war piece imagined as from the mouth of the "Unknown Soldier." He described as lies the atrocity stories about the enemy in World War I. The battle scenes with the piles of smashed bodies in the big picture book were bad enough. Mary Elizabeth quickly put her hands over her eyes after the first glance and refused to look again. But the book also placed in front of us photographs of rows of Belgian babies spitted on the bayonets of grinning, helmeted German soldiers. Bare-breasted women writhed in chains that bound them to cannons. Mr. Bill had mentioned those exact examples of allied "propaganda." Having made myself look at all the pictures, I sampled the reading. The enemy now seemed to be not the already powerful Nazis but the powerful Communists. The editors warned that those who wished to divide the wealth of the world and those who wished to disarm it were the same people.

All my life I had wanted nothing so much as to believe in my father's rightness and courage, and mostly I had. Comparing the message of his latest merchandise, however, with what I had heard at school, I was dismayed. In forcing himself to sell this awful book, making himself believe that it was a great and truthful book, he was degrading himself as he never had been degraded before. Of course he would never have completely agreed with my teacher, a man probably fifteen years younger than he, who had not had his experiences. But one of the reasons I liked my history teacher was that he had so much in common with Daddy, the same vigorous intelligence and enthusiasm that assured us that learning really mattered. I believed that if my father had recently studied World War I, without having the book to sell, his ideas would have changed.

I could see that it was not a time to speak up, and if I was especially quiet, no one noticed. Daddy remained at home for several days to become completely familiar with the book, and to try selling it at the schools which were within easy driving distance of McKenzie. I got another attack of asthma, which I was having frequently that fall, and as I was sitting up in bed I listened to him practice the sales talk that he would give to high school history teachers, principals, and American Legionnaires.

Apparently not running into Mr. Bill, he felt sure that he was going to make his first sale at McKenzie High School. The two or three Legionnaires he visited may have been the first men in McKenzie that he had spoken to as friends since we moved to town and they seemed genuinely interested in the book. In the end the school did not take the book. Maybe Mr. Bill did get to the principal after all. Daddy made two or three sales in towns not far away by giving up his commission, working more for less money than even on the gas stove gadgets. All the belief he had to bring to it could not make a success of that book. We all felt lucky that before Christmas he was able to switch over to the sale of school equipment: desks and chairs, globes and maps.

Christmas in high school meant preparation for mid-term examinations after the holiday more than it meant name drawing and present giving, although there was a Christmas tree on the stage of the big room that served both for an auditorium and the study hall. We sang Christmas carols at the weekly chapel instead of "The Old Oaken Bucket" and "John Brown's Body."

On the day when school was finally dismissed, John B. went with Mother to cut our Christmas tree in a neighbor's field, and they returned just as snow began to fall. Mary Elizabeth nailed together the crosspieces for a stand and secured the tree in its place. While Mother was popping corn, John B. had hunted up the box of ornaments from other years and was pushing us all to get the tree decorated. He was the biggest enthusiast about Christmas I have ever known except maybe Mother. Then we heard some stamping on the porch and suddenly there at the front door was Daddy with his arms full of his big box. We were all at the door at once. Then Daddy was inside and the box he was carrying was on the floor. Maybe this time, maybe this time, Daddy had come home with some presents. It was for him, not us, that we wanted him to have them. But right away we could see that something was wrong: "That car! I was on the edge of town when it went dead again. I spent a day in a garage in Union City last week and thought I had it fixed." He sent Mary Elizabeth and John B. to pick up some other things at the garage where another motorist had helped him push the car.

Mother built up the fire so Daddy could warm himself and went into the kitchen to start preparing supper early. Caroline and I kept on putting ornaments on the tree.

"How were the pigs this week, Daddy?" I asked, although he looked as though he didn't want to talk at all.

"Oh, the pigs were pigs," he said.

He had come home during the week of school vacation both for Christmas and because nobody was on the job in the schools to sell equipment to. I could see that he was really worried about the car.

Caroline, small for her age, still had kittenish ways. She wound a piece of paper chain around Daddy's ear and her arms around his neck, "Want to be a Christmas tree? I'm glad it's Christmas so you could come home."

Mother came rushing in from the kitchen, "Is there enough wood on the fire?" She noticed Caroline fooling with Daddy's ear. "Don't bother Daddy, Caroline. He's tired." Daddy smiled his one-sided smile and put the chain on Caroline's head like a crown. Mother saw it was all right and went back to her work in the kitchen.

It wasn't a bad Christmas. I had begun grading papers for teachers at school and working on the school newspaper for which the National Youth Administration paid me ten cents an hour. I was spending a dollar, not a dime, on each member of the family, and Mother had helped me select very carefully just what was needed most. Mary Elizabeth, Caroline and John B. had all found ways to make a little money. Mary Elizabeth still did not touch the money saved in the bank to buy a bicycle.

The next time Mother came in to look at the fire, I knew what Daddy was going to say before he said it, "Sweetheart, I'd like us to get by on as little as we can this Christmas." He and Mother had agreed on that every year since the end of the oil boom. Then he explained why: "I am going to have to do something about that car before I get out of town."

"The children are growing up," said Mother. "They are buying things for each other this year."

"Well, I hope you aren't counting on me," said Daddy. "I don't have any more this year than I did last."

He didn't mean to sound harsh. We all knew he was miserable. He kept on being miserable all Christmas, sitting much of the time with his head in his hands. There were a few happy hours when he played dominoes and *Monopoly* with us. He and John B. both loved *Monopoly*. Daddy was almost as glad for John B. to win, as to win himself.

A day or so after my fifteenth Christmas, except for Daddy and me everybody was out of the house. I was wheezy enough so Mother had told me to stay in bed while she was over at her biscuit lady's cleaning up her Christmas mess. Who knew? Maybe the old lady would give us some dried out fruit or some squeezed chocolates nobody wanted. (That was my thought—not Mother's.) Daddy sat by the fire trying to read Booth Tarkington's *Penrod and Sam* which I had brought him from the library. I can't remember what I was reading. It was not *Uncle Tom's Cabin* which would have reminded me of some Simon Legree beating Daddy to death.

I felt sure that Daddy's selling for the school equipment company wasn't going to work. He needed to work with big things and important people, as in oil or insurance or maybe bonds, if I knew what bonds were. Or he could work with little things and little people as when he sold the gas stove gadgets. Back at the University of Texas he had been a great success selling popcorn—teasing, cajoling, entertaining. I knew he thought that by selling school equipment he was combining his two skills of teaching and selling; I could see why the company hired him. But as for his patience at sitting outside pompous school superintendents' offices while they scolded restless kids for throwing paper wads, that would soon run out. He could be charming to anyone if he was feeling good, but on a low day, he could make a self-confident school official feel ignorant. That person would always find the school budget didn't allow money for new equipment this year, which it probably didn't.

Daddy couldn't absorb himself in his book. Eventually he put it down and began looking at the fire. I put down my book and began to look, too. When the rustle of the bed sheets indicated that I had moved, he looked up and crinkled his eyes in almost a smile.

"T. ('T', his diminutive for 'U.T.'), you can be sure that I married your Mother because I knew she would make a good mother for my children."

I didn't know what to say.

What was he trying to tell me? Why was he telling me this? I vaguely nodded my head, not quite able to say, "And she has, too," or "She's that and a lot more."

"Don't ever forget that," he said, moving his head firmly up and down. We both went back to reading.

Those moments came back to me after he left and did not return: Had he already made up his mind then that he might not be coming back? Was he telling me, the oldest of the four, who would be grown first, that he had the highest regard for Mother? She could be (Granddad's favorite word) *"depended* on." However it might look, we children were not being abandoned.

The next day at the garage Daddy was told that he shouldn't put another cent into his old car. They would give him $50 on it toward another that would run. If he could come up with $100 in cash, he could pay off the remainder of the cost at $5 a week.

Daddy did not talk to his children about family financial concerns as Mother was likely to, but of course he told her about the offer and she told me.

"Where in the world will he get that much money?" I asked.

"Now just don't worry about it," Mother said. "It'll come."

In the days after Christmas, Daddy spent less time at home and more out in the community. I thought maybe he was trying to stir up more interest in that World War I book. But I soon learned that he was going to all those friends we had made in the community—the widows, old maids and some wives—and borrowing $5 here and $10 there. Mrs. Thorne must have received several dollars in the mail one day, because he got $10 from her, and he went out on the edge of town through the iron gate and between the dark fir trees and introduced himself for the first time to Miss Edna as "U.T.'s father." At Aunt Grace's I'll bet they talked about several of each other's favorite books, and Mother got some money from her Sewing Room friend, and even the biscuit lady. When he had collected all he needed except for the last $30, he asked Mary Elizabeth to make a trip to the bank with him to take out her chicken money, and of course she couldn't refuse. In fact she looked happy and as though she felt good to be doing it as they went out the door. When she had closed her little savings account, she walked with him to the garage to pick up the car and she had the first ride in it.

Mrs. Thorne had been coming to our house for dinner on New Year's Day ever since she told us that in Middle Tennessee they ate black-eyed peas and hominy on the first day of the year for "peace and harmony" all year round. Mother said, "It would take some well-off people like you folks in Middle Tennessee to think something as common as that makes a New Year's dinner. But if that's all we need, we'll have it, and corn bread, too."

Dinner that day was the first meal since we came to McKenzie where Daddy sat down with a guest at a meal. Mother mentioned later that she thought he and Mrs. Thorne would have more in common now that she had loaned him some money. In the blessing before the meal, Mrs. Thorne kept telling the Lord what a wonderful family we were. Then she kept telling Daddy the same thing all during the meal. He smiled a little, but the spirit of play to meet her mild coquetry wasn't in him.

He drove away on January 2 to try his fortune in a new year.

Chapter IV

After January 1936

A few times when I came home from school after Mother's day working at the Sewing Room she met me to say, "I feel like Daddy John has been thinking about us today." Mother's instantaneous decision not to go with the car dealer to Memphis to make inquiries at the time of his disappearance was characteristic of the way she continued to behave. She did not want Daddy to come home until he was ready and she continued to believe that he would fulfill the promise of his note, "I'll make good yet."

For the first year there was no word from him and no word from anyone who had seen him since his car was picked up. We all wanted to tell him that he did not have to make so terribly good. Eventually, we learned from Social Security that he had applied for a Social Security number at an office in Brooklyn, New York in April 1937, a little more than a year after he left home. This was proof that he had not committed suicide in the earlier despairing time, as he had promised Mother he would not. But no money had ever been placed in the Social Security account and none taken out. As to date of death, the Social Security document sent to us recorded "1937?" with the question mark included.

We all went to Sunday School and church the Sunday after that sad Saturday in 1936, and to school on Monday. No one asked us about Daddy and we did not tell anyone. In my third-year high school English class we were actually reading the American Transcendentalists. The words of Thoreau and Emerson became a kind of private memorial for me. At least at one time our father had been Thoreau's "sturdy lad from New Hampshire or Vermont [I read 'Texas'] who in turn tries all the professions, who teams it, farms it, peddles, keeps a school…." He was also Emerson's "Every man": "The power which resides in him is new in nature, and none but he knows what that is that he can do until he tries." I took for myself Thoreau's "If you have built your castles in the air your work need not be lost; that is where they should be."

Mother and Daddy had taken for granted that college for the

children was as essential as our own beds, piano lessons, and library books when we were little. Throughout our childhood we heard again and again Granddad's statement about not stopping "this side of Harvard or Yale." Then in seventh grade there were the parallel sentences: "He was an *alumnus* of Yale. She was an *alumna* of Vassar." Mother remembered that Frances McVey, the suffragist leader and wife of the president of the University of Kentucky, had been a Vassar graduate. Before high school I received a Vassar catalogue and carefully chose for my courses those required for admission. Within weeks of the time Daddy left I sent the next ten-dollar check earned on NYA for an application for early admission to Vassar and the second check for an application for two College Board examinations to be taken the summer after junior year. It never occurred to Mother that I should use the money for anything else. She was not surprised when I passed the exams and was granted the early admission. Her faith was strong in "Ask and ye shall receive" for modern as well as biblical times, especially for her children. Then Boyce Alexander Gooch (Vassar '15) came into our lives in the spring and summer of 1937.

When I needed the recommendation of a Vassar alumna to apply for a scholarship, the Vassar Admissions office sent me the name of Frances Coe, the president of the Memphis Vassar Club, who passed my letter on to Mrs. Gooch. She was able to track me down through a phone at the house of next-door neighbors. Caroline and John B., playing in the yard on a bright April day, yelled up to me in our second floor apartment.

I heard both the South and the city in Mrs. Gooch's voice when she told me that she was going East to visit Vassar soon, and that she might be able to help me. She would pay my bus fare to Memphis if I would come the following Saturday.

From the moment I got off the bus at 123 E. Parkway N. and a maid in a white cap and apron opened the front door of the Georgian brick house at the end of a long brick walk, everything went smoothly. "Pearl, this is Miss U.T.," said Mrs. Gooch, not stumbling over my odd name. The very dignified woman about my mother's age was already wearing a hat and gloves for the lunch party she had planned with three Vassar alumnae. One of them was Miss Willie C.

Johnson (Vassar '95), a teacher who had encouraged Mrs. Gooch to go to Vassar.

The phone call came again when I passed the additional College Boards in the summer and was offered a $500 college scholarship. A day later when we were upstairs trying on clothes, Mrs. Gooch told me: "Of course, you have my Willie C. Johnson Scholarship." Since McKenzie was a hundred miles from Memphis, it was natural for me to stay with the Gooches when I came to town. On this second visit Mr. Gooch told me about his first job cutting logs at a dollar a day in Grayson County, Kentucky, not far from our grandfather's farm. He met Mrs. Gooch in Arkansas when she was teaching in the neighborhood of his lumber business. After they were married, his first Christmas present to her was an annual Vassar scholarship for a recent high school graduate.

With no children of her own Mrs. Gooch had some of her best times buying clothes for her nieces, Jean and Marie Alexander, and for other young women she sponsored. For me, it was an entire wardrobe, along with everything else she thought I needed. By the time I finished college, my teeth would be straightened.

A major event of my leaving for college was having my wardrobe trunk taken off the train in McKenzie and hauled up to our house so that I could show my new clothes to family and friends. Mary Elizabeth and Caroline have always claimed that they were more stunned than envious. Mrs. Thorne, who had made it clear that being good and doing good was more important than any college, used her full vocabulary of adjectives as sweaters, suits, an evening dress and each pair of shoes came out of the trunk. Miss Edna disapproved of Mrs. Gooch's choice of bright colors for me (she liked to see me in blue and white), but still insisted on buying my railroad ticket to Poughkeepsie, New York.

The Gooches did not meet Mary Elizabeth until after she had spent her senior year in high school at Aunt Pearle's in Dimmitt, Texas. Without having met her, they paid her tuition for the Bowling Green College of Business in the fall of 1939. Mrs. Gooch asked me to bring her with me when I came to visit during the Christmas of my junior year. Mary Elizabeth charmed everybody including the servants and their dog named Gumbo. Before the next year was over she was on her way to the University of Kentucky with her trunk full of clothes.

Mother never met Mrs. Gooch, but it was at her request that Mrs. Gooch called Caroline and told her that she could not go to Vassar if she married at sixteen. Caroline insisted that she and her ministerial student boyfriend hoped to go to South America as missionaries; she graduated from high school valedictorian of her class and pregnant. After a divorce from her first husband and the death in an automobile accident of her second, the war hero Bill Blakely, she returned to Bethel College with five children and her valedictorian's scholarship. She graduated summa cum laude in 1958. My brother John B. became "John" when he went into the army after he graduated from high school. Having survived the war, he graduated from the University of California at Los Angeles with help from the GI Bill of Rights.

The satisfactoriness of their relationship with Mary Elizabeth, me and other young people, including Mrs. Gooch's nieces, had a part in the Gooches' establishing in 1943 the C. M. Gooch Foundation. During the thirty-five years of its existence it gave 12,000 loans and scholarships for further education to high school graduates in the areas where Mr. Gooch had made his money in lumber: West Tennessee, eastern Arkansas, and northern Mississippi. When the foundation was liquidated, the remaining capital was distributed to the educational institutions the Gooch students had chosen in proportion to the numbers who had chosen them. The largest amount went to the University of Tennessee in Martin, about 25 miles from McKenzie. Very few students from the area designated by Mr. Gooch chose Vassar, the institution with which the program had begun.

The money Mother received when she started working at the Sewing Room, about $20 a month, covered the rent, the light and water bills, and the small amount we spent for groceries. But we were all glad when the sewing project was replaced by a WPA literacy program. For about the same amount of money Mother went around town hunting out adults, some of whom she and Mrs. Thorne had already come to know, who were willing to spend time learning to read and write. As it was almost impossible to get them together in groups, she walked to their individual homes and naturally became involved in their lives. She was as strict with them about reading and writing as she thought was reasonable. She also taught them basic health rules and about making birthday cakes, dyeing Easter eggs, and trimming Christmas trees.

As the nation prepared for war in the early '40s school jobs began to open up. There was no demand for women ministers so Mother went back to teaching. Through the employment office of the Teachers' College in Bowling Green, to which she and Daddy still owed money from the '20s, she found successive positions in Kentucky, Georgia, Kentucky again, and Ohio. She then made a great leap west to Henderson, Nevada. Her last schools were in the state of Washington which had a particularly good teachers' retirement plan.

Payment of family debts was a major objective of Mother's second teaching career. On visits back to Kentucky and Tennessee, she looked up the shoe repairman and all the grocery men to whom the family owed money and tried to pay every debt no matter how small. Anna and Ernest now owned the farm and she did not feel so guilty as earlier about Granddad's having to pay off the $1000 loan to Cousin Wash Brown. After Granddad died in 1944, she began giving Grandmother $25 a month. She was also very proud of being able to build a "home of her own" in Kosmos, Washington, a tiny community where she was surrounded by Kentuckians and Tennesseans who had gone west to work in the lumber camps. Whatever the local denomination in all those places where she lived she taught Sunday School. If there was no Sunday School, she started one.

Although her daughters and son wanted to believe that Mother was content with her very productive life, she remained conscious that she had not accomplished what she had set out to do. Never mind that most of the white Protestant denominations did not begin allowing women in the ministry until the 1950s and that the Cumberland Presbyterian Church, which had pioneered with the ordination of women, called few women. She had not become a minister.

In 1957 when my professor husband received a Guggenheim Fellowship, our family went to England for the year. Mother, retired from teaching, came with us. She lived near Westminster College, the distinguished Presbyterian seminary that is part of Cambridge University, and attended classes. When we all returned to the United States, she made a brief visit to her home in Washington state, and then resettled in McKenzie. There she re-enrolled at the Bethel Seminary and persuaded Dr. William Ingram, a fellow theological student of the '30s, now a professor in the seminary, to direct the dissertation which she had begun more than twenty years before: "Doctrine of Reconciliation, the Theological Basis of Christ's World Mission." In 1960 my three children and I attended the ceremony where at the age of 68 she received the degree that is now called "Master of Divinity." Wearing her cap and gown and holding her diploma in her hand she said: "Of course, I will never preach now, but I had to finish what I started."

In 1964 the Cumberland Presbyterian Theological Seminary left Bethel College in McKenzie and moved to Memphis as the Memphis Theological Seminary of the Cumberland Presbyterian Church. Dr. Ingram was one of its first new presidents, and it was he who in 1987 helped to set up the Mary Elliott Miller Award to be given each year to outstanding women recipients of the Master of Divinity degree. "She deserves it," he said. "She was a pioneer." Twenty-three women received the Mary Elliott Miller Award at Memphis Theological Seminary between 1987 and 2005. The woman who received it in 2005 was in a class of 24 women and 17 men.

If Mother was not complacent about what she had achieved, she also refused to give more credit to us children than she thought we deserved. As long as she could speak, she added the names of her fifteen grandchildren, eight boys and seven girls, to her nightly prayers. But she never bragged that she had given birth to four college graduates. She was proud that John had fought for his country and that Caroline had done valuable work for Dr. Frank Laubach's "Each one, teach one" organization, the Foundation of World Literacy. But the four of us had not become the "writer, artist, musician, and minister" that she had told us she wanted when we were children. She granted that Mary Elizabeth had been useful to her husband Stanley Lampert, a successful lawyer and businessman, and that Joe Summers had written good books on George Herbert and John Milton. But those were their successes and not ours. I, in particular, should have done more.

McKenzie celebrated Mrs. Thorne's seventy-ninth birthday, on February 24, 1959, which Mayor Y. D. Moore proclaimed as "Eula Thorne Day" in honor of the 54 years of service to McKenzie in which she had "joyfully and unselfishly given her time, strength and love to the community." When I last visited her in 1963, the year before she died, her straight back was bent almost double. The bank had long since foreclosed on her house and she had given up her white clothes in favor of anything anyone gave her that she could wear. She lived upstairs in a small apartment of friends close enough to the major churches. She called for me to come on in when I tapped at her door. She was removing from the oven corn bread that she made twice a week for the wild birds she fed. Almost mischievously, I asked her what kinds of birds she attracted. "Heavens, darling," she said, "I haven't the slightest idea. Sparrows, I suppose."

Before the final stages of Alzheimer's, when Mother could still talk, she could figure out a way to turn any place into the farm in Kentucky where she had grown up. A piece of paper in a hedge was a chicken. The neighbors' red-wood fence in a Michigan suburb became the fence around the old orchard where Granddad kept pigs. She was confused about all of us. Her daughters were likely to be either "Mother" or her beloved sister "Edna." She remembered her father as a giant. Whenever we saw something especially grand and new—a shiny shopping plaza, an intricately constructed cloverleaf on a thruway or an airport with an impressive perspective, she would spread out her arms, "You know my father built all of this." Then, "I've never seen a country change like this one."

Our father became dimmer and dimmer in her mind. I hadn't heard her mention his name for a long time when she shuffled into the kitchen one morning in her bedroom slippers and housecoat: "Did you ever hear what became of John B. Miller?"

"No, I never heard," I said.

"Wasn't he a kind of fly-by-night?"

There was room in the family plot in the Little Bend, near Grandmother and Granddad, Uncle Henry, Evie, and Edna for Mother to be buried, when she died in February 1976. Point Pleasant Church was in a good state of repair because many people loved it and had prospered enough to take care of it. In the early Kentucky spring the daffodils were in bloom.

Mother's sister, Anna, took responsibility for the arrangements as she had for Grandmother and Granddad. Our brother John drove with all his family from Mexico. Caroline required two cars from Syracuse, New York, for her large family and for Jeanne Higgins, a Syracuse neighbor who had taken care of Mother in her home for several years. The pall bearers were four grandsons and two nephews. Many of the old friends, neighbors, and students, even some relatives I did not remember, gathered at the funeral home in Beaver Dam. We heard again, "Miss Mary—there never was a teacher like her." Mother had selected years before the text that would go on the little headstone above her grave: "As for me and my house, we will serve the Lord" (Josh. 24:15).

"Hold tight, Sweetheart. I'll make good yet." It was at the Miller-Elliott reunion in Arlington, Texas, Thanksgiving weekend 1996, that the question about the postal card came up once more. My brother John and his daughter Jackie with her family had recently moved into the elegant house on Ledbetter Street that Jackie's husband, John Greason, had built. Along with about fifty of the Miller-Elliotts of four generations, Judge Jack Miller, the son of Daddy's brother, Uncle Goodwin, and Sue and Anne, daughters of his sister Aunt Pearle, were there. In an attempt at the closure which had never quite occurred, we lighted three candles for the third birthday of Jackie's son, John Kristopher, and 100 candles for the hundredth birthday, October 19, of his great-grandfather, John Brison Miller.

Caroline, Mary Elizabeth, and John, three of the four children of John Brison Miller and Mary Elliott Miller, named sons for Daddy. I kept the name "U.T." which continued to feel like a gift from him. Nobody except our father himself could give his family his humor, intelligence, and love of his West Texas family and us. But our continued love was also a gift of Mother's love and the awe in which she held the name "Father."